TWAYNE'S WORLD LEADERS SERIES

EDITOR OF THIS VOLUME

Samuel Smith, Ph. D.

Quintilian As Educator

MARCUS FABIUS QUINTILIANUS

Quintilian As Educator

Selections from the *Institutio Oratoria* of
MARCUS FABIUS QUINTILIANUS

Translated by

H. E. BUTLER

Edited with Introduction and Notes by
FREDERIC M. WHEELOCK, Ph.D.

Twayne Publishers, Inc. New York

Copyright © 1974 by Twayne Publishers, Inc.
All Rights Reserved

Library of Congress Cataloging in Publication Data

Quintilianus, Marcus Fabius.
   Quintilian as educator.
   (Twayne's World leaders series)
   1. Quintilianus, Marcus Fabius. I. Butler, Harold
Edgeworth, 1878- tr. II. Title.

LB91.Q7413 1974   370.1   73-14903
ISBN 0-8057-3596-0

MANUFACTURED IN THE UNITED STATES OF AMERICA

Preface

The permission of the Harvard University Press to use H. E. Butler's translation of Quintilian in the Loeb Classical Library is here gratefully acknowledged. This is a translation in the twentieth-century idiom; and if it is at times interpretative rather than literal, it reads more easily and gains clarity. The peculiarities of punctuation such as the excessive use of colons and the at times sparse use of commas cause no real problem.

The following system of citing and locating passages has been used: the large Roman numerals refer to the twelve books of the *Institutio Oratoria;* the small Roman numerals refer to the chapters in those books; and the Arabic numerals indicate the sections within the chapters.

It is hoped that the selected passages will prove relevant to the general modern reader even though they may be presented by Quintilian under the heading of Roman oratory. The attempt has been made to adapt the passages via headings in the text and commentarial footnotes even to those who have had little or no experience with the classical tradition and via various obiter dicta intended to emphasize important points in the text or to provoke the reader, be he parent, teacher, student, or general reader. A certain amount of repetition has been deliberate.

Books I and II, undoubtedly the most interesting, have been presented in major part. They cover the curricula and studies of pre-school, elementary, secondary, and higher education and give a picture of a fine liberal arts education with literature as its cornerstone. In addition to the subject matter, one can find here paragraphs dealing with methods and motivation, and with principles that anticipate some modern ones. Other sections discuss the ideal teacher (the moral and intellectual excellence and the humanity, without undue permissiveness, to be required of teachers); teacher-student relations and the needs of students themselves; the problem of irresponsible, ambitious, and even corrupt parents; the insistent gospel of hard work and many exercises necessary to build the firm foundations for the requisite excellence in language written or oral; repeated emphasis on good morality to be learned through literature and repeated denunciation of all sham and ostentatious display. And there are many other interesting and instructive insights awaiting the reader. The brief excerpts from the remaining books were chosen because they effectively reinforce important points already made, such as the paramount value of reading and what to read; the invaluable benefits of careful composition and how to compose; the need of a large, accurate vocabulary and of wise memorization. Finally, Book XII states that most desirable above all else is the acquisition of a good character formed by philosophy and reason with the aid of good literature.

Through Quintilian's authoritative and humane work of nineteen hundred years ago we can acquire a beneficial historical perspective about moral and intellectual values, about well-disciplined expression, and about details of education which can substantially point the way to the correction of some of the weaknesses in our own educational systems and can make for more intelligent living and citizenship. In the words of Dr. Samuel Smith, "The present generation will make truly practical and wise decisions if they delve into their heritage so that, while avoiding historical errors, they will preserve those elements of human experience which have proved to be beneficent."

I am deeply grateful to my wife, Dorothy, for her faithful preparation of the manuscript and for her many helpful suggestions. My thanks also go to Dr. Samuel Smith, editor of the series, for his kind encouragement and guidance and valuable suggestions.

Contents

Preface	
Chronology	
Introduction	1
Life of Marcus Fabius Quintilianus	2
Outline of Greek Education	3
Outline of Roman Education	8
Purpose and Nature of Roman Education	14
Influence and Tradition of Quintilian	17
Bibliography	19
Letter to His Publisher	21
Book I, Preface	22
Book I, Chapters i-xii (Elementary and Secondary Education)	29
Book II, Chapters i-xiii, xvi, xix, and xxi (Higher Education)	79
Book III, Excerpts from Chapter i (Origin and Types of Oratory)	122
Book IV, Excerpts from Chapter ii (Excellence in Communication of Facts)	125
Book VIII, Excerpts from Preface and Chapter ii (Vocabulary Enrichment and Clearness in Style)	128
Book X, Excerpts from Chapters i, iii, iv, v, vii (Reading and Writing)	130
Book XI, Excerpts from Chapter ii (Memory)	145
Book XII, Excerpts from Chapters i, ii, and xi (The Character of the Ideal Orator)	148
Index	153

Chronology

First Century B.C.—First Century of Our Era

B.C.
106-43	Marcus Tullius Cicero: orator, patriot, statesman, author.
102-44	Gaius Julius Caesar: statesman, general, genius.
96-55	Lucretius, author of *De Rerum Natura (On the Nature of Things)* on Epicurean philosophy and an atomic theory.
84-54	Catullus: lyric poet.
63	Conspiracy of Catiline, thwarted by Cicero.
60	First Triumvirate: Caesar, Pompey, Crassus.
58-51	Caesar's conquest of Gaul.
55-44	Cicero wrote widely on philosophy, political science, and rhetoric, including obiter dicta on education.
49-44	Dictatorships of Julius Caesar.
44	Caesar assassinated on Ides of March.
43	Second Triumvirate: Antony, Octavian, Lepidus; Cicero proscribed and assassinated for Philippics against Antony.
31	Battle of Actium: Octavian defeated Antony and Cleopatra.
27	Octavian, given title of Augustus, became first Roman emperor, ruled well until his death in A.D. 14.

QUINTILIAN

4	Birth of Jesus Christ.
	Leading literary figures of the Augustan period:
70-19	Virgil: author of *Aeneid,* most famous Roman national epic.
65-8	Horace: famous satirist and lyric poet.
59-A.D.17	Livy: author of epic-spirited history of Rome.
43-A.D.17	Ovid: most famous for hexameter work on mythology entitled *Metamorphoses.*

A.D.

14-37	Reign of Tiberius, conscientious but moody emperor.
26-36	Pontius Pilate, procurator of Judaea.
37-41	Reign of Caligula, mad emperor.
41-54	Reign of Claudius, weak emperor, not personally vicious.
43	Conquest of southern Britain.
54-68	Reign of Nero, egotistical, vain, devoted to literary pursuits and art, corrupt, cruel, finally detested.
64	Great fire at Rome; persecution of Christians.
65	Conspiracy of Piso against Nero, and consequent deaths of Seneca and many others.
68	Revolts against Nero, who finally took his own life.
68-69	Brief reigns of successive emperors: Galba, Otho, Vitellius.
69-79	Reign of Vespasian: efficient, honest, decent.
70	Destruction of Jerusalem by Titus, Vespasian's son.
70	Professorships established by Vespasian; Quintilian held one of these.
79-81	Reign of Titus, a good emperor.
79	Eruption of Vesuvius destroyed Pompeii and Herculaneum.
81-96	Reign of Domitian, brother of Titus: good administrator but autocratic, suspicious, sensual.
90	Quintilian retired.
96-180	Era of the "five good emperors": Nerva, Trajan, Hadrian, Antoninus Pius, Marcus Aurelius.

Chronology

Some important literary figures of the first century:

4-65	Seneca: Stoic philosopher, essayist, dramatist; tutor of the young Nero.
23-79	Pliny the Elder: military and public leader, omnivorous reader and compiler, author of encyclopedia.
ca.35-95	Quintilian.
45-104	Martial: author of witty and satirical epigrams.
ca. 46-120	Plutarch: Greek author of moralia and biographies of famous Greeks and Romans.
ca.62-113	Pliny the Younger: pupil of Quintilian, orator, public servant whose gentle and kindly letters reveal decency and humanity of best Romans of his time.
55-117	Tacitus: orator and writer on oratory but most famous as satirical historian of imperial period.
ca.55-127	Juvenal: author of vitriolic satires against evils of his time.

Introduction

Quintilian's educational doctrines, promulgated nineteen hundred years ago, represented the best thinking of the ancient world concerning education and culture. These doctrines reflect the ideals and practices of his time, as, for example, in their emphasis upon skills of communication and rhetoric, essential elements of higher education in the Roman Empire. Yet, Quintilian's educational philosophy was surprisingly modern in tone and character, antedating by nearly two millennia our contemporary respect for the rights and needs of children; and many of his views on learning, ethical training, and child development deserve to be studied and implemented in education today.

Students of the history of education attest to the lasting value of Quintilian's contributions to educational theory and practice.

Thus, Wilds and Lottich state that Quintilian's work constitutes "the first practical exposition of the entire field of education . . . also the first real approach to a solution of the problems of educational methodology . . . the first treatment of the principles of educational procedure, and anticipates many of our so-called modern principles of teaching. . . ." (Elmer H. Wilds and Kenneth V. Lottich, *The Foundations of Modern Education* [3d ed.; New York: Holt, Rinehart and Winston, 1961], p. 96.)

J. Wight Duff writes that Quintilian "proved himself to be one of the great educators. . . . Many of the eternal principles of a sound education are to be found in him stated for all time with convincing authority. The fact that many of his pronouncements retain their applicability amidst modern problems of teaching is, like the constant citation of his critical dicta, among the proofs of his permanent value." (*A Literary History of Rome in the Silver Age* [New York: Charles Scribner's Sons, 1927], p. 409.)

And J. F. Dobson comments: "Fortunately for us [Quintilian] held, in contrast to most writers on the subject, that the way in which the twig is bent will determine the growth of the tree; and where others had been used to take for granted the studies pursued in early stages before the pupil came under the tuition of the *rhetor,* he considers that nothing, however trivial, should be neglected.... [He] considers education as a whole from the very beginning." (*Ancient Education and Its Meaning to Us* [New York: Cooper Square Publishers, Inc., 1963], p. 134.)

LIFE OF MARCUS FABIUS QUINTILIANUS

Although it is difficult to be definitive about many of the details of Quintilian's life, the following outline will suffice for our purposes. Born in the Roman province of Spain about A.D. 35, Quintilian received his education under the leading teachers and orators at Rome, where his father was a successful teacher of rhetoric. At some point after completing his education, Quintilian returned to Spain as a teacher of rhetoric, only to be brought back to Rome in A.D. 68 by Galba, the governor of Spain, who became Roman emperor for a few months during that turbulent year following the death of Nero (emperor A.D. 54-68). In further evidence of his success and merit as a teacher can be cited St. Jerome's statement that "Quintilian was the first to have a public school and to receive a salary from the imperial treasury, and he became famous." The imperial treasury was undoubtedly that of the emperor Vespasian (A.D. 69-79). Finally, after twenty years of teaching and oratory in the courts he retired about A.D. 90 and devoted himself to the writing and publishing of his famous *Institutio Oratoria,* the *Education of an Orator* (see the letter to his publisher Trypho and also Book I, Preface, §§ 1 ff.). During this period both additional honor and tragedy fell to the lot of Quintilian: honor in his being appointed by Domitian (emperor A.D. 81-96) to be the tutor of the two grandsons of Domitian's sister, as he tells us in Book IV, Preface,§ 2; tragedy in the deaths of his young wife and two sons, which he poignantly recounts in §§1-16 of the preface to Book VI. The *Institutio Oratoria,* Quintilian's only extant work, was published about A.D. 95. Twice (VI.Pref.3; VIII.vi.76) he mentions his somewhat earlier but now lost book on the *Causes of the Corruption of Eloquence,* which interests us in the light of his frequent protests in the *Institutio Oratoria* against the decadent characteristics of the rhetorical practices of his times. The exact date of Quintilian's death has not been determined, but a likely possibility is ca. A.D. 100.

Not only are we interested in Quintilian's life but we also want to know what kind of person he was. Since our author constantly reveals his nature and personality throughout his work, there is no need at this point to do more than list a number of his characteristics, for which the reader will be finding corroborative evidence as he peruses the work itself and through which the reader can feel that he has come to know a fellow human being who happened to live nineteen hundred years ago. A man of wide teaching experience, Quintilian was devoted to professional and academic excellence; he was very conscientious and competent, thorough and exacting but fair. He believed in honest hard work and uncompromising discipline (i.e., instruction and training), which alone would lay the firm and enduring foundations necessary for any lasting superstructure of later accomplishment. In all this he was as demanding of teachers as he was of students, for he felt that teaching should be regarded as a calling and a profession, not a mere dollars-and-cents job. He despised shoddiness, sham, ostentation, conceit, extravagance, and vulgarity in teachers, parents, and students alike; and he was equally ready to praise and reward whatever was good, whatever was laudable. He was sound, sane, sensible, practical, reasonable, a man of good judgment, who believed in proper balance and the "golden mean," who was open-minded toward the present but conservative of past good. We find him kind, patient, understanding, and humane; and he was a tender family man. We admire him for his constant insistence on high standards of morality and for his earnest and enthusiastic devotion to his ideal of the high calling of the orator-statesman, who must be first of all a good man. In sum, we see in Marcus Fabius Quintilianus a human being of attractive personality, an experienced master teacher, a fine humanistic gentleman and scholar.

Outline of Greek Education

Since Roman education, like so much else in Roman civilization, came to be tremendously influenced by Greek education, we obviously cannot fully understand Quintilian's position in this field without some idea of Greek theory and practice.

The earliest evidence for education in our occidental tradition comes from the epic poet Homer (ca. eighth century B.C.), who in the *Iliad* and the *Odyssey* depicts the civilization of the heroic age of some centuries before his own time. He has Phoenix, the tutor of youthful Achilles, say that he was sent to Troy by Achilles' father to make Achilles "a speaker of words and a doer of deeds." "A speaker of words" refers to oratory; and in Achilles, Odysseus, Nestor, and others Homer provides examples of oratory in the public assembly and even among friends. Hence we see that, from the beginning, debate and oratory were very important in Greek experience. Achilles is also shown chanting epic lays to the accompaniment of the lyre, a scene which tells us something about the composition, memorization, and musical delivery of epic literature in the heroic age. All this foreshadows the conspicuous place of literature, music, elocution, and rhetoric in later Greek education. Also Homer's accounts of well-developed athletic contests foreshadow the role of gymnastic activity in the later Greek curriculum.

By the early fifth century we can see how education has become more or less systematized. At Doric Sparta, for example, the schools were public and were completely controlled by the state; attendance was compulsory for all the children of Spartan citizens; the cirriculum was almost entirely physical and militaristic and aimed at making every citizen a superb soldier totally subservient to the state, since the Spartans, a small conquering minority of a few thousand, lived and ruled like an armed camp amid a vanquished and embittered majority many times larger. This is an example of education responsive to a situation.

Fortunately, however, in the general Greco-Roman educational tradition the free Ionic-Athenian spirit prevailed. At Athens education was private and democratic. Fathers sent their sons to private schools of their own choosing and paid the tuition (at least down into the fourth century). School attendance was by choice of the people universal through the age of about fourteen; but it was voluntary in that it was not required by the state, except that, if a father failed to provide his son with an education, the son did not have to support him in his old age. Although not all the details of Athenian education in the early fifth century are completely clear, the main features may be sketched as follows.

Introduction

The preschool period (ages one to six) shows the importance of the parents and the nurse. Says Plato: "Education and admonition commence in the first years of childhood, and last to the very end of life. Mother and nurse and father and tutor are vying with one another about the improvement of the child as soon as he is ever able to understand what is being said to him; he cannot say or do anything without their setting forth to him that this is just and that is unjust; this is noble and that is base; this is pious and that is impious; do this and don't do that. And if he willingly obeys, well and good. If not, he is straightened by threats and blows, like a piece of bent or warped wood. At a later stage they send him to teachers and enjoin them to see to his manners even more than to his reading and music" (Plato, *Protagoras* 325.c-d, Jowett's translation). Obviously morals and manners and religion were stressed in this preschool period. Then when the child was sent off to school, he was attended by a *paedagogus* ("child leader"), a trusty slave who was not a schoolteacher (as our derived word "pedagogue" implies) but a constant guardian responsible for the child's manners, respect for elders, moral conduct, and general well-being.

We now come to the basic primary education for all boys from the age of about six to fourteen. (Although the girls at Sparta received a good education of its kind, the Athenians were not very much concerned about a girl's education outside of the home.) This curriculum the Athenians divided into two parts: *mousike (techne)* and *gymnastike (techne)*. "Music," any art or skill *(techne)* presided over by the Muses, comprised in the present instance various intellectual pursuits, especially those connected with many aspects of language and literature as well as music in our sense. "Gymnastic" obviously indicates the serious, thorough physical training and athletic contests for which the Greeks were so famous. Thus the Athenians contrived to train both the mind and the body.

In school the earliest years were directed to the three R's: the alphabet, phonics, writing, dictation, elementary reading, memorization and proper recitation of select passages of poetry, and simple arithmetic via fingers and abacus. Then after the mastery of the three R's there was extensive reading of the poets, both epic and lyric. The teacher explicated the texts with special emphasis on their ideals and moral value, and the pupils memorized and recited with appropriate delivery hundreds of lines, especially from Homer, who was thought to be the greatest teacher of all (and is still held to be one of the immortals). Continuing the passage from the *Protagoras* above, we read: "And when the boy has learned his letters and is beginning to understand what is written, as before he understood only what was spoken, they put into his hands the works of great poets, which he reads sitting on a bench at school; in these are contained many admonitions and many tales and praises, and encomia of ancient famous men which he is required to learn by heart in order that he may imitate or emulate them and desire to become like them. Then, again, the teachers of the lyre take similar care that their young disciple is temperate and gets into no mischief, and when they have taught him the use of the lyre, they introduce him to the poems of other excellent poets, who are the lyric poets; and these they set to music, and make their harmonies and rhythms quite familiar to children's souls, in order that they may learn to be more gentle and harmonious and rhythmical, and so more fitted to speech and action; for the life of man in every part has need of harmony and rhythm. Then they send them to the master of gymnastic, in order that their bodies may better minister to the virtuous mind and that they may not be compelled through bodily weakness to play the coward in war or on any other occasion. And the more socially influential people are the more they go in for that, and the richest are the most influential. Their children begin to go to school soonest and leave off latest."

The last two sentences indicate that the children of families of modest means ended their education with the primary curriculum outlined above, which was the basic educational experience common to all the citizens in the democracy, but that the children of the more well-to-do continued their education in what we might call the secondary school (ages ca. fourteen to eighteen), where they would have more advanced study of literature, language (e.g., grammar, rhetoric, meter), mathematics, geometry, and the like. This secondary education seems to have developed after the Persian Wars (490-479 B.C.) with the increasing affluence and influence that attended the growth and power of the Athenian empire in the latter half of the fifth century.

At the age of eighteen the young Athenian entered on his two-year period of military training and garrison duty, at the end of which he became a full-fledged Athenian citizen. After this, if

Introduction

he had the means and time, he could continue his education by studying under the Sophists and also later, from the fourth century on, under the philosophers as well (cp. Plato's Academy and Aristotle's Lyceum). This would provide the equivalent of our higher education.

The Sophists were originally itinerant professors who gravitated from Asia Minor and Magna Graecia to the center of power and wealth in the second half of the fifth century B.C. to meet the new educational needs at Athens; and initially, at least, many of them, like Protagoras above, were men of fine repute. For a fee they lectured on various topics such as practical virtue and ethics, literature as a good general education for success in public life, polymathia (broad learning), disputation, memory training, language study, rhetorical skills, and oratory. In the last analysis, these lectures and courses were directed toward practical success in a democratic society where success depended so greatly on skillful, persuasive oratory and debate of all sorts in political life, in the courts, on public occasions, and in the governance of the democracy's newly acquired empire. Since their prime aim was to teach how to succeed at all costs, they were not concerned about standards of right and wrong (i.e., they were amoral); and so they argued that the individual should not only be well educated but also should be his own free judge of morality. Thus they became careless and skeptical about the olden virtues and values. They challenged and upset the long accepted beliefs and morality to the extent that, says Aristophanes in the *Clouds,* they could teach a person how to prove any point—even that the wrong was right and the right was wrong. Socrates and Plato also deplored the irresponsibly eristic excellence of the Sophists. Such criticism implies that, although the Sophists started out as amoral, the influence of some, at least, must have become immoral. However, the careful and critical study of language, rhetoric, and oratory and the concept of higher education and broadened curricula owed much to the Sophists.

The great Socrates, though sometimes linked superficially with the Sophists, differed from them fundamentally in that he was concerned with positive (not relative) virtue and right action and moral responsibility rather than merely selfish, expedient, practical, successful conduct and action. In education he is most famous (1) for his "dialetical" or "Socratic" method of question-

and-answer discussion with his followers, which led to ever improved, more exact definitions and so more accurate concepts of true virtue, justice, beauty, etc.—he sought to teach men to think more clearly; and (2) for his emphasis on morally right action rather than mere expediency, on good character rather than worldly success.

Finally, through his philosophical descendants (Plato, Aristotle, the Stoics, and the Epicureans), Socrates can be regarded as the father of the philosophical schools of the fourth century and the following Hellenistic period. These college-like institutions systematized and disseminated knowledge and theory, and they made Athens the intellectual center of the world down into Roman times long after Athens had lost all political influence to Rome. There were also the Hellenistic universities like that famous one at Alexandria (founded 283 B.C.), which, with its tremendous library and scholars in residence, was intended less for teaching than for research in literature, mathematics, science, medicine, and natural history. Among the schools of rhetoric the most renowned was that of Isocrates (436-338 B.C.), who because of personal handicaps became a teacher of oratory rather than an actual orator. He taught elegant rhetorical composition in all styles and, like Quintilian, he stressed the improvement of natural ability through training, hard work, perseverance, and good character. Later rhetorical instruction was less distinguished and was directed more to school exercises than to life.

It was this Greek system of primary, secondary, and higher education with all its emphasis on language, literature, rhetoric, philosophy, morality, music, mathematics, geometry, and gymnastic which impressed the Romans during their early contacts with the Greeks in the third century B.C. and which the politically victorious Romans subsequently adopted in large part and adapted as their own. Such is the Greek setting for Quintilian.

Outline of Roman Education

First Period of Roman Education (ca. 500-250 B.C.). While the Athenian state and its system of education were developing so rapidly during the fifth century B.C., Rome was a primitive little city-state, a mere pinpoint on the Tiber River, not yet in complete control even of the people immediately surrounding her. Not until after many vicissitudes and the Pyrrhic victories of the Greek general Pyrrhus and the surrender in 272 B.C. of the Greek city of Tarentum in southern Italy to the Romans, can Rome finally be regarded as mistress of Italy proper from the Arno and Rubicon rivers southward. During this native Roman period, before the great tide of Greek influences spread over Rome, Roman education was a practical utilitarian affair taught by the father of the family. It comprised the rudimentary Latin three R's and also instruction in ancestral customs, religion, morality, patriotism, physical and military fitness, and the general activity about the homestead. The reason for the lack of any real literature in the Roman curriculum of this period (as we saw the strong literary tradition in Greek education stemming early from Homer et al.) was the fact that the Romans had no such great literature to turn to as did the Greeks.

Second Period of Roman Education (ca. 250-100 B.C.). Through victorious political and military ventures eastward during this second period the Romans were brought into sustained contact with Greek culture and education, by which they were captivated despite the opposition of conservatives like Cato. Symbolic of all this is Livius Andronicus, a Greek from Tarentum, who was taken to Rome as a slave and was subsequently given his freedom. He was probably the first schoolmaster to introduce the Greek tradition into Roman education, for according to Suetonius "he taught privately and publicly in both languages" (i.e., Greek and Latin); and finding no good textbook for the subject of literature, which was so important in the Greek system, he translated Homer's *Odyssey* into Latin and this long remained a textbook.

Thus to the native Roman primary education Andronicus added the Greek literary element which was to develop rapidly thereafter into a secondary curriculum under the *grammaticus,* who would teach composition (including grammar) and reading in Greek literature and Latin literature, as that developed, and other subjects which had given the literary cast to Greek education. Later other famous Greeks visited Rome as ambassadors or hostages and gave lectures and training in Greek rhetoric and oratory, which were now in growing demand, especially for the training of Roman politicians and the officials who were being sent out to administer the authority which was expanding throughout the Mediterranean. This curriculum of the rhetoricians with the addition of some philosophy supplied the equivalent of our higher education. We need not be concerned with all the details and sometimes conflicting evidence of how the Greek influence permeated Roman education. It is enough to note that these Greek elements did coalesce with the Roman to produce the system which became relatively standard during the next period of Roman education from ca. 100 B.C. to A.D. 100.

Third Period of Roman Education (ca. 100 B.C. - A.D. 100). Since the Roman educational system changed little in form during this two-century period and since Quintilian is our greatest and fullest authority on this period, we can rely on his text for the details. Consequently, at this point a brief outline will suffice for a synoptical view of the immediate system and the completion of our survey of Greco-Roman education through Quintilian.

A. PRIMARY, OR ELEMENTARY, EDUCATION: AGES CA. 6-12. (See Quintilian, Book I, Chapters i-iii.) Somewhat informally Quintilian includes the preschool period (up to the age of six or seven) under the heading of primary education, for he believes that education should begin as soon as possible in the home under the parents and the child's nurse. If, for example, the nurse were Greek, as so often was the case, the child could from the outset learn the rudiments of speaking Greek as well as Latin; and via games he might even learn some ABC's. Then, as the boy entered the primary school proper, he would according to the Greek custom be given a *paedagogus,* who performed the same general services as he did for the Greek boy above, and in addition he might help the Roman boy continue with his conversational Greek. Under the *ludi magister,* Latin for "schoolmaster," the boy completed his knowledge of the alphabet and worked on syllables, pronunciation, writing, reading of selections from good literature, much memorization of maxims and moral or heroic passages, and arithmetic. This process must have been much like the earlier native Roman education only somewhat more literary, a sound basic education. No doubt many sons of the poorer people would leave school for work at this point.

As among the Athenians, school attendance was voluntary but general; and the schools were private in that they were supported through the relatively small tuition charges paid by the parents, who were free to make their own choice of schools. Classes of the

Introduction

primary schools were ordinarily held in some portico or open room. They were noisy; and for furniture they commonly had not much besides benches for the students and a chair for the teacher. Punishment in both Greek and Roman schools was regularly administered in the form of flogging, which the humane Quintilian roundly condemned. Though there was some program of physical exercise, the exercises were apparently not as thoroughly organized as among the Greeks. The evidence for the education of girls beyond what they could receive at home is not clear, but they seem to have had at least a minimum of primary education and some had more than that.

B. SECONDARY EDUCATION: THE SCHOOL OF THE GRAMMATICUS: AGES 12-16. (See Quintilian Book I, Chapters iv ff.) Those who were in a position to do so entered the secondary school to study under the *grammaticus*. The very use of the Greek word reflects the now established acceptance of the Greek influence in Roman education since the grammaticus taught his Roman pupils Greek grammar, language, literature (poetry), etc. along with, of course, the Latin equivalents. Thus the educated Romans became bilingual by early training and education, as the Greeks never were. The Greeks would learn foreign languages for utilitarian purposes of trade but did not study them in school for their cultural and literary value because, for understandable reasons, they regarded their own language and literature as superior. This new approach, then, is an important contribution of the Romans to educational theory, viz., the idea that the study of foreign languages and literatures has a valid and valuable place in the curriculum of a liberal education; and this tradition has survived beneficially down to our own times. To be sure, it is today being severely challenged by the less sensitive and less understanding educationists, but one sincerely hopes that we shall continue wise enough to grant at least a reasonable place to foreign languages and literatures in the liberal arts program. The details of the secondary curriculum are set forth by Quintilian in Book I, iv. ff., under such headings as language, grammar, correct speaking and writing; literature (especially poetry), explication of texts (covering such topics as mythology, history, philosophy, astronomy); memorization; recitation of texts with attention to delivery; composition; qualities of style; and music, geometry, and astronomy. There is evidence that, if a boy was not in a position to continue on to the full higher education of the school of the rhetor, he could toward the end of his secondary program receive some training in the introductory exercises of rhetoric and thus gain some experience of a complete well-rounded education. Incidentally, the Greek influence mentioned above is further evidenced by the fact that the Romans used the Greek word *schola,* meaning "leisure (for intellectual pursuits)," to refer to the "school" of the grammaticus or the rhetor, whereas the word for the more native elementary Roman school was *ludus,* meaning "game or sport," and the elementary teacher was called by the thoroughly Latin name of *ludi magister.*

C. HIGHER EDUCATION, SCHOOL OF THE RHETOR: AGES CA. 16—. (Books II ff.). When a boy reached about the age of sixteen, he laid aside his crimson-bordered toga of boyhood, donned his white toga of manhood *(toga virilis),* and was enrolled as a full Roman citizen. This was the time for the young Roman who wanted a higher education to enter the school of the rhetor and study rhetoric in earnest. Both "rhetor" and "rhetoric" derive from the same Greek root, which means "to speak." Consequently rhetor is the etymological equivalent of Latin *orator,* "pleader, speaker"; and rhetoric by a little extension comes to mean the art and practice of the effective use of language in writing and speaking. Immediately there comes to mind the great importance of oratory in the democratic political life at Athens and the consequent place of rhetoric in the Athenian curriculum, especially under the influence of the Sophists. Similarly in republican Rome there was an ever increasing need of rhetorical and oratorical power in public life: in the public assemblies and the Senate, in elections and deliberations, in the courts, and in the administration of Rome's growing imperial power. Accordingly, the already well-developed skill of the Greeks in this field was eagerly adopted by the Romans as indicated above. In the days of the Republic down through the Ciceronian period this was a genuine, free, viable, disciplined oratory used in debate, attack, defense, the determination of public policy. However, the probably inevitable establishment of the monarchical empire in the first century of our era meant very severe, if not fatal, restrictions on the erstwhile free democratic institutions. Thus, no matter how fine some of the emperors were, the fact remained that imperial sensitivity and blight gradually impaired the élan vital of oratory,

Introduction

while at the same time the formal system of rhetorical training continued to dominate Roman education. Quintilian vehemently protests against the resultant shallowness, affectation, extravagance, and ostentatious display in the commonly empty oratorical exercises of his period; but nonetheless he demonstrates the undeniable value of well disciplined, effective expression and shows how it can be attained through a sound rhetorical curriculum of broad humanistic compass which includes extensive reading in oratory, poetry, history, philosophy, and especially Livy and Cicero, always with emphasis on good character.

For the student of the first century B.C. there were formal treatises and courses on oratory dealing with the three types of orations (deliberative, forensic, public ceremonies), the various steps and devices in the preparation of a speech, exercises and declamations, innumerable technicalities of language and delivery. Such points are, of course, also covered in the more technical portion of Quintilian's *Education of an Orator;* but more important, Quintilian goes far beyond the mere bones of technical treatment and provides wise and interesting methods, insights, advice, and ideals which are valid for us today in our concern about better education and better language.

After his graduation from the school of the rhetor our young Roman might round out his education by a postgraduate trip to such intellectual centers as Athens, Rhodes, Pergamum, and Alexandria for advanced study of rhetoric and philosophy under the leading scholars of the day. One of the best examples of this is Cicero's two-year period of study in Greece and Asia Minor.

The system of liberal arts and rhetoric outlined above continued through the rest of the Roman Empire except that it gradually declined toward academic and rhetorical formalism; and, although it became less closely connected with life, it did stand for the intellectual activity of its times.

In the triumph of Christianity, the church was often hostile toward pagan education even though such great men as St. Jerome and St. Augustine had received a classical rhetorical education. However, the church did realize its need of Latin; and the cultivation of the Trivium (grammar, logic, and rhetoric) and the Quadrivium (music, arithmetic, geometry, and astronomy), i.e., the Seven Liberal Arts, in the monastic schools and the universities clearly reflected the continuing influence of the Roman educational tradition even if the Seven Liberal Arts now lacked much of the inspiration of the ancient humanism, and Scholasticism's primary interest was otherworldly, i.e., metaphysical.

With the decline of Scholasticism and the advent of the Renaissance in the fifteenth century came the rebirth of interest in the ancient classical literature and rhetoric and in the classical humanistic views concerning man in this world (i.e., in ethics rather than metaphysics). During the next four centuries the classics held a chief, at times tyrannous, place in our curricula until science and other subjects challenged the classics in the nineteenth century. Now the pendulum has swung to the opposite extreme, which in its materialism and technology is far too often antihumanistic, if not anti-intellectual. Let us hope that the pendulum will soon come back to a middle position since all men, scientist and humanist alike, sorely need the linguistic discipline of rhetoric in the best sense and the inspiration of great literature, as said our Quintilian.

Purpose and Nature of Roman Education

Any history of education will quickly convince us that the purposes and nature of education vary with the time, the place, and the circumstances. What then were the purposes of Roman education in the period of ca. 100 B.C.-A.D. 100?

In Cicero's *Commonwealth (De Republica,* I.xx) Mucius asks, "What then do you think we ought to study in school, Laelius?" Laelius replies, "Those subjects which would make us useful to the state." Be it noted that this was not a declaration for a system of education controlled by a monolithic, totalitarian state where the state was all and the citizen was nothing but a slave to the state, as for instance in Sparta; it was the educational ideal of a republic, where the free person could have his own individual rights and goals in life but where those ideals could be achieved only in the cooperative effort and the well-being of the society in which he lived. This meant a liberal education especially in literature and rhetoric for the inextricably intertwined advantages of both the the individual and the state; and the higher education was no doubt most commonly pursued as an aid to a career in public service. Good citizenship was good for the state and for the individual.

Introduction

Some 145 years after the above quotation from Cicero's *Commonwealth,* Quintilian cited Cato's famous description of an orator as a *vir bonus dicendi peritus,* "a good man skilled in speaking" (XII.i.1); and in his preface to Book I Quintilian states his aim thus: "My aim, then, is the education of the perfect orator. The first essential for such an one is that he should be a good man, consequently we demand of him not merely the possession of exceptional gifts of speech, but of all the excellences of character as well.... The man who can really play his part as a citizen and is capable of meeting the demands both of public and of private business, the man who can guide a state by his counsels, give it a firm basis by his legislation and purge its vices by his decisions as a judge, is assuredly no other than the orator of our quest." (I.Pref.§§9-10.) Certainly Quintilian did not expect that every citizen could be an ideal, consummate orator-statesman and that everyone would require training in all the technical details which he sets forth in Books III-XII; but Quintilian did believe that his basic curriculum could benefit all citizens in two ways.

Following the order in Cato's epigram above, Quintilian says that the prime essential beyond all else is *good morality, good character;* this is the greatest and most important thing, the sine qua non. An education which does not emphasize and seek to inculcate good morals is positively dangerous and pernicious (XII.i.1).

The second essential is *rhetoric,* Cato's "skilled in speaking." At the outset let us not think of rhetoric as something quite artificial and stultifyingly formal, for it can be defined simply as the study of the effective use of language or the art of clear, accurate, and skillful expression in speaking and in writing, an art crucially important in the communication of ideas. Quintilian says that the Creator gave to the other animals many gifts which man does not possess, but he gave to man the special advantages of reason and speech. However, marvelous as is the power of reason, it cannot be very helpful without the ability to express thoughts adequately in words (II.xvi.12-15,17). For a person may have the greatest ideas in the world, but if he cannot express them effectively and convincingly to his fellow men, these ideas can accomplish little. Hence the importance of rhetoric for the ancient Roman citizens—and, by the way, for modern Americans.

By what curriculum, then, could the two essentials of character and rhetoric be accomplished? Quintilian believed that both goals could be achieved through a broad humanistic, liberal arts curriculum, a basic education for all—though there might be some variety in the courses according to special bents and not all might choose or be able to complete the rhetor's full curriculum of higher education (II.viii.7). In Quintilian's view literature, which would include grammar and other linguistic studies, was the foundation of a liberal education (I.iv.5). He reasoned thus: the three essentials for forceful speaking (i.e., rhetoric) were reading, writing, and speaking, all so inextricably interconnected that no one of them could be neglected (X.i.1-2). Reading supplied models and vocabulary for practice in writing and so became the pilot in composition (X.i.2f.). Since frequent practice in composition was "the best producer and teacher of eloquence," as Cicero said (X.iii.1), the power of eloquence ultimately derives from reading. Accordingly literature, or reading, constituted the cornerstone of Quintilian's educational system. "Unless the foundations of oratory are well and truly laid by the teaching of literature, the superstructure will collapse" (I.iv.5).

Furthermore, literature (e.g., all branches of Greek and Latin poetry, history, philosophy, and oratory) was no less important in the paramount matter of character (morals) indicated above; for by the reading, analyzing, and memorization of great literature the student gained ideas and sentiments and philosophies and examples of great heroes, actions, characters, and ideals which should be imitated, and also examples of others which should be avoided. Thus literature would mold a boy's character and would provide a thesaurus upon which to draw throughout life. In sum, "the study of literature is a necessity for boys and the delight of old age, the sweet companion of our privacy and the sole branch of study which has more solid substance than display" (I.iv.5).

The modern reader may think it a defect that in Quintilian's curriculum there is an absence of vocational or mechanical courses and that there is no real study of science except for what theories one might gain from certain "natural" philosophers. In slave-owning societies, where slaves performed many of the menial and manual tasks and any free men similarly employed would learn their work on the job, it was the tradition that education should be liberal (i.e., befitting a free man, a *liber*) and should be based on what Cicero called the "liberal arts," subjects suitable for free men, which included literature and language, rhetoric, philosophy, music, mathematics, geometry, and astronomy. Though the list might vary somewhat, literature and rhetoric predominated. Such is the origin of the liberal arts curriculum, which with some variations and additions has survived down to our twentieth century, sometimes under the name of the humanities in contradistinction to the sciences. The rather stupid and dangerous split between "the two cultures" of the scientific and humanistic-literary communities, "which can't or don't communicate," is the subject of C. P. Snow's *The Two Cultures: And A Second Look*, in which he states the belief that science and the literary tradition will simply have to unite. In this direction it is heartening to read (in a recent issue of *Time* magazine) of the increasing popularity of the humanities at the Massachusetts Institute of Technology, to the point that growing numbers among the four thousand science and engineering students are electing to take considerably more humanities courses than they are actually required to take and that the literature classes are swamped, which is a hopeful sign of the recognition of the good that is traditional in addition to the good that is new. Says the Institute's President Jerome B. Wiesner, "A person is much less of a human being if he thinks of himself only as a technocrat. Society needs the cognitive reaction of a poet as well as a technologist"; and he expresses the hope that this will be a "renaissance in which man will replace machine at the center of the stage." This is the spirit of humanism and liberal arts.

Influence and Tradition of Quintilian

Quintilian's wide experience and fame, his appointment to the first Roman professorship by Vespasian and to the tutorship of two princes in Domitian's household, and the requests which he received for the publication of the *Institutio Oratoria,* all point to the acceptance and influence of Quintilian in his own time. The poet Martial puts it thus (II.90.1-2):

> Quintiliane, vagae moderator summe iuventae,
> Gloria Romanae, Quintiliane, togae.

"O Quintilian, noblest guide of flighty youth, thou glory of the Roman toga." However, after his death he and his Ciceronianism seem to have suffered some academic opposition from the linguistic faddists of the period and perhaps some loss of popularity for a time. Then in the fourth century Julius Victor wrote an *Ars Rhetorica,* which follows Quintilian very closely; and Quintilian appears as one of St. Jerome's favorite pagan authors, and St. Augustine, originally a professor of rhetoric himself, certainly knew him. The encyclopedists Cassiodorus (A.D. 480-575) and Isidore of Seville (A.D. 570-636) kept Quintilian's name clearly alive. Just because there follows a long period with no specific mention of Quintilian, we do not have to conclude that there was no knowledge of Quintilian during that time; for in the ninth century Lupus Servatus (A.D. 800-863), an ardent classicist and humanist with a knowledge of many classical authors, wrote to the Pope asking for a copy of the full twelve books of the *Institutio Oratoria,* saying that he had only incomplete copies of the work.

After another lacuna in recorded reference to Quintilian, we come to the cathedral school at Chartres, where John of Salisbury (in the twelfth century) was educated in a program which was dominated by Quintilian's methods. In the thirteenth century encyclopedist Vincent of Beauvais was familiar with Quintilian's text. Petrarch by the middle of the fourteenth century was very enthusiastic about his coming into possession of even an incomplete copy of the *Institutio Oratoria,* and he wrote an admiring "letter to Quintilian."

As the rediscovery and revival of all the other classical authors inspired the enthusiastic and dedicated humanists of the Renaissance, so Poggio's exciting discovery of the entire twelve books of Quintilian at St. Gall inspired the humanistic educators, such as Vittorino da Feltre, Aeneas Silvius Piccolomini, Guarino da Verona, Laurentius Valla, Pomponius Laetus, Erasmus, and Juan Vives. Quintilian's influence here was enormous, in educational theory and in his emphasis on literature, language, and morality. In the sixteenth century Martin Luther regarded Quintilian as an excellent authority on education. Similarly in England evidence of Quintilian's influence can be seen in Thomas Elyot's *Governor* and Richard Mulcaster's *Positions* during the sixteenth century, and Ben Jonson's *Discoveries* in the seventeenth century. Alexander Pope in the eighteenth century attests his indebtedness in this couplet from his *Essay on Criticism:*

> In grave Quintilian's copious works we find
> The justest rules and clearest methods join'd.
> (Part III.669-670.)

Among those who read Quintilian in the nineteenth century can be named Benjamin Disraeli, Thomas B. Macaulay, and John Stuart Mill. These names as well as the others cited above form only the top of the iceberg. Writers on rhetoric and composition in the nineteenth and twentieth centuries refer to Quintilian. Certainly many unknown others were helped by Quintilian but never bore extant written testimony to the fact; and certainly many educational theories and curricular details in modern times have reflected the influence or the parallelism of Quintilian's great work even when the fact is not admitted. Be that as it may, Quintilian's *Institutio Oratoria* is still capable of inspiring us and helping us as one of the noblest and soundest works in pedagogical and humanistic literature.

Bibliography

Translations of the entire twelve books.

Butler, H. E. *Institutio Oratoria of Quintilian with an English Translation,* 4 vols. Cambridge, Massachusetts: Harvard University Press; London: William Heinemann Ltd., Loeb Classical Library Series, 1920-1922, and reprinted variously to 1969.

Watson, John Selby. *Quintilian's Institutes of Oratory: or, Education of an Orator,* Literally Translated with Notes, 2 vols. Bohn's Classical Library, 1856; subsequently reprinted by George Bell and Sons, London, 1891.

Selections in translation.

Little, Charles E. *Quintilian the Schoolmaster,* 2 vols. of translation and paraphrases. Nasvhille: George Peabody College for Teachers, 1951.

Murphy, James J., ed. *Quintilian, On the Early Education of the*

Citizen-Orator. Books I-II.10, Watson's translation. Indianapolis: Bobbs-Merrill Co., Library of Liberal Arts Series, 1965.

Smail, William. *Quintilian on Education, Being a Translation Selected Passages*. Originally Oxford: Oxford Univer Press, 1938; New York: Teachers College Press, Columt. University, as of 1969.

Commentaries.

Colson, F. H. *M. Fabii Quintiliani Institutionis Oratoriae. Liber I.* Latin text of Book I with notes and accounts of Quintilian's life, Roman education of his times, his own educational theories and influence. New York: Cambridge University Press, 1924.

Peterson, W. *M. Fabii Quintiliani Institutionis Oratoriae Liber Decimus.* Latin text of Book X and accounts of Quintilian's life and literary criticism. New York: Oxford University Press, 1891.

On Roman Education.

Dobson, J. F. *Ancient Education and Its Meaning to Us.* New York: Cooper Square Publishers, Inc., Our Debt to Greece and Rome Series, 1963.

Gwynn, Aubrey. *Roman Education from Cicero to Quintilian.* Oxford: The Clarenton Press, 1926. Reprinted New York: Russell and Russell, 1964.

Wilkins, A. S. *Roman Education.* Cambridge, England: The University Press, 1905.

****

Barr, Donald. *Who Pushed Humpty Dumpty? Dilemmas in American Education Today.* New York: Athenaeum, 1971. (Mr. Barr is a keen, no-nonsense, stimulating, well-balanced analyst of the educational ferment and problems of our times, who in innumerable ways echoes or parallels Quintilian. This book can be recommended as a must for all who are concerned with and about education.)

LETTER TO HIS PUBLISHER[1]
Marcus Fabius Quintilianus to His Friend Trypho,[2] Greeting

You have daily importuned me with the request that I should at length take steps to publish the books[3] on the Education of an Orator which I dedicated to my friend Marcellus.[4] For my own view was that they were not yet ripe for publication. As you know I have spent little more than two years on their composition, during which time moreover I have been distracted by a multitude of other affairs. These two years have been devoted not so much to actual writing as to the research demanded by a task to which practically no limits can be set and to the reading of innumerable authors. Further, following the precept of Horace who in his Art of Poetry deprecates hasty publication and urges the would-be author.

"To withhold
His work till nine long years have passed away,"
I proposed to give them time, in order that the ardour of creation might cool and that I might revise them with all the consideration of a dispassionate reader. But if there is such a demand for their publication as you assert, why then let us spread our canvas to the gale and offer up a fervent prayer to heaven as we put out to sea. But remember I rely on your loyal care to see that they reach the public in as correct a form as possible.

1. This letter and the translations in succeeding chapters are reprinted by permission of the publishers and the Loeb Classical Library from H. E. Butler, tr., *Quintilian, Institutio Oratoria, Books I-IV, VIII, X-XII*, Cambridge, Mass.: Harvard University Press.

2. This letter shows that Trypho was a trusted publisher at Rome. His name would indicate that he was of Greek extraction.

3. The plural "books" (*libros* in Latin) refers not to various different works by Quintilian but to the fact that his *Institutio Oratoria (Education of an Orator)* was published in the form of twelve "books" roughly corresponding to our "volumes." In §1 Professor Butler's translation actually has the singular "book" for Quintilian's plural *libros*, apparently to stress the fact that this is one work, as is indicated by the title. However, in § §2-3 Professor Butler abruptly changes to the plural which Quintilian's text requires ("them," "their," and "they"). In the interests of clarification and consistency the corresponding singulars of §1 ("book," "it was," and "its") have here been changed to Quintilian's plurals ("books," "they were," and "their").

4. Marcellus Victorius is little known beyond what Quintilian tells us in section 6 of the preface to Book I.

MARCUS FABIUS QUINTILIAN
ON
The Education of an Orator
BOOK I
PREFACE

1-3. After twenty years of teaching experience, Quintilian was urged by his friends to undertake the present work in the hope of arbitrating the contradictory opinions of numerous Greek and Roman writers on education. He finally acceded, thinking that he might in the process introduce something new.

Having at length, after twenty years devoted to the training of the young,[1] obtained leisure for study, I was asked by certain of my friends to write something on the art of speaking. For a long time I resisted their entreaties, since I was well aware that some of the most distinguished Greek and Roman writers[2] had bequeathed to posterity a number of works dealing with this subject, to the composition of which they had devoted the utmost care. This seemed to me to be an admirable excuse for my refusal, but served merely to increase their enthusiasm. They urged that previous writers on the subject had expressed different and at times contradictory opinions, between which it was very difficult to choose. They thought therefore that they were justified in imposing on me the task, if not of discovering original views, at least of passing definite judgment on those expressed by my

---

1. Note that Quintilian is writing out of his own experience and practice as a veteran teacher, not as a mere theorizing neophyte.
2. Among them Aristotle and Cicero; and many others are named by Quintilian *passim*.

The Education of an Orator Bk. I, Preface

predecessors. I was moved to comply not so much because I felt confidence that I was equal to the task, as because I had a certain compunction about refusing. The subject proved more extensive than I had first imagined; but finally I volunteered to shoulder a task which was on a far larger scale than that which I was originally asked to undertake. I wished on the one hand to oblige my very good friends beyond their requests, and on the other to avoid the beaten track and the necessity of treading where others had gone before.

4-6. Quintilian could contribute something new because almost all the other writers on the art of oratory despised the preliminary stages of education or thought that they were not their concern or, what is nearer the truth, had no hope of making a gratifying display of their talent in dealing with subjects which are far from being showy. Quintilian, however, will begin with all the elementary stages and go through the entire process of education aiming at the perfect orator.

For almost all others who have written on the art of oratory have started with the assumption that their readers were perfect in all other branches of education and that their own task was merely to put the finishing touches to their rhetorical training; this is due to the fact that they either despised the preliminary stages of education or thought that they were not their concern, since the duties of the different branches of education are distinct one from another, or else, and this is nearer the truth, because they had no hope of making a remunerative display of their talent in dealing with subjects, which, although necessary, are far from being showy:[3] just as in architecture it is the superstructure and not the foundations which attracts the eye.

I on the other hand hold that the art of oratory includes all that is essential for the training of an orator, and that it is impossible to reach the summit in any subject unless we have first passed through all the elementary stages. I shall not therefore refuse to stoop to the consideration of those minor details, neglect of which may result in there being no opportunity for more important things, and propose to mould the studies of my orator from infancy, on the assumption that his whole education has been entrusted to my charge.

---

3. Throughout the entire work Quintilian vehemently denounces ostentation, affectation, and extravagance in any form. See also notes 15, 36, *et passim* below.

This work I dedicate to you, Marcellus Victorius. You have been the truest of friends to me and you have shown a passionate enthusiasm for literature. But good as these reasons are, they are not the only reasons that lead me to regard you as especially worthy of such a pledge of our mutual affection. There is also the consideration that this book should prove of service in the education of your son Geta, who, young though he is, already shows clear promise of real talent. It has been my design to lead my reader from the very cradle of speech through all the stages of education which can be of any service to our budding orator till we have reached the very summit of the art.

9-13. The ideal orator must possess excellences of character as well as of speech; and Cicero regarded the same man as uniting in one person the qualifications of orator and philosopher.

My aim, then, is the education of the perfect orator. The first essential for such an one is that he should be a good man, and consequently we demand of him not merely the possession of exceptional gifts of speech, but of all the excellences of character as well. For I will not admit that the principles of upright and honourable living should, as some have held, be regarded as the peculiar concern of philosophy. The man who can really play his part as a citizen and is capable of meeting the demands both of public and private business, the man who can guide a state by his counsels, give it a firm basis by his legislation and purge its vices by his decisions as a judge, is assuredly no other then the orator of our quest.[4] Wherefore, although I admit I shall make use of certain of the principles laid down in philosophical textbooks, I would insist that such principles have a just claim to form part of the subject-matter of this work and do actually belong to the art of oratory. I shall frequently be compelled to speak of such virtues as courage, justice, self-control; in fact scarcely a case comes up in which some one of these virtues is not involved; every one of them requires illustration and consequently makes a demand on the imagination and eloquence of the pleader. I ask you then, can there be any doubt that, wherever imaginative power and amplitude of diction are required, the orator has a specially impor-

---

4. For a similar and inspiring picture of the ideal orator as a good man see Book XII.i.25-31. One would like to think that the education which produces such a man must have in it elements good for the more ordinary citizen (though not in the same rhetorical detail required for the orator).

The Education of an Orator   Bk. I, Preface

tant part to play? These two branches of knowledge were, as Cicero has clearly shown, so closely united, not merely in theory but in practice, that the same men were regarded as uniting the qualifications of orator and philosopher.[5]

13-15. Then this combination of oratory and philosophy split apart with certain adverse results.

Subsequently this single branch of study split up into its component parts, and thanks to the indolence of its professors was regarded as consisting of several distinct subjects. As soon as speaking became a means of livelihood and the practice of making an evil use of the blessings of eloquence came into vogue, those who had a reputation for eloquence ceased to study moral philosophy, and ethics, thus abandoned by the orators, became the prey of weaker intellects. As a consequence certain persons, disdaining the toil of learning to speak well, returned to the task of forming character and establishing rules of life and kept to themselves what is, if we *must* make a division, the better part of philosophy, but presumptuously laid claim to the sole possession of the title of philosopher, a distinction which neither the greatest generals nor the most famous statesmen and administrators have ever dared to claim for themselves. For they preferred the performance to the promise of great deeds. I am ready to admit that many of the old philosophers inculcated the most excellent principles and practised what they preached. But in our own day the name of philosopher has too often been the mask for the worst vices. For their attempt has not been to win the name of philosopher by virtue and the earnest search for wisdom; instead they have sought to disguise the depravity of their characters by the assumption of a stern and austere mien accompanied by the wearing of a garb differing from that of their fellow men.

16-20. As we all frequently deal with those things which philosophy claims for its own, so let our ideal orator be such as to have a genuine title to the name of wise man (philosopher), not only blameless in character but also master of the science and art of speaking.

Now as a matter of fact we all of us frequently handle those themes which philosophy claims for its own. Who, short of being an utter villain, does not speak of justice, equity and virtue? Who

---

5. Cicero's *de Oratore* III.15. In olden times the same teachers formed the morals and the language, as, for example, did Achilles' tutor Phoenix in Homer. Cp. Quintilian II.iii.12 below and note 20 thereon.

(and even common countryfolk are no exception) does not make some inquiry into the causes of natural phenomena? As for the special uses and distinctions of words, they should be a subject of study common to all who give any thought to the meaning of language. But it is surely the orator who will have the greatest mastery of all such departments of knowledge and the greatest power to express it in words. And if ever he had reached perfection, there would be no need to go to the schools of philosophy for the precepts of virtue. As things stand, it is occasionally necessary to have recourse to those authors[6] who have, as I said above, usurped the better part of the art of oratory after its desertion by the orators and to demand back what is ours by right, not with a view to appropriating their discoveries, but to show them that they have appropriated what in truth belonged to others. Let our ideal orator then be such as to have a genuine title to the name of philosopher: it is not sufficient that he should be blameless in point of character (for I cannot agree with those who hold this opinion): he must also be a thorough master of the science and the art of speaking, to an extent that perhaps no orator has yet attained. Still we must none the less follow the ideal, as was done by not a few of the ancients, who, though they refused to admit that the perfect sage had yet been found, none the less handed down precepts of wisdom for the use of posterity. Perfect eloquence is assuredly a reality, which is not beyond the reach of human intellect. Even if we fail to reach it, those whose aspirations are highest, will attain to greater heights than those who abandon themselves to premature despair of ever reaching the goal and halt at the very foot of the ascent.

21-22. Brief table of contents by books.

I have therefore all the juster claim to indulgence, if I refuse to pass by those minor details which are none the less essential to my task. My first book will be concerned with the education preliminary to the duties of the teacher of rhetoric. My second will deal with the rudiments of the schools of rhetoric and the problems connected with the essence of rhetoric itself. The next five will be concerned with Invention, in which I include Arrangement. The four following will be assigned to Eloquence, under which head I include Memory and Delivery. Finally there will be one book in

---

6. For a detailed statement about the orator's need to study philosophy see, for instance, XII.ii.1,4,6-8 (especially §8).

The Education of an Orator   Bk. I, Preface

which our complete orator will be delineated; as far as my feeble powers permit, I shall discuss his character, the rules which should guide him in undertaking, studying and pleading cases, the style of his eloquence, the time at which he should cease to plead cases and the studies to which he should devote himself after such cessation.

23-25. The method of teaching is to be set forth under each topic in such a way as not only to impart to students the laws of rhetoric but also to nourish their eloquence. For as a rule the dry, supersubtle textbooks kill the subject by providing the mere bones and not giving them a covering of vital flesh.

In the course of these discussions I shall deal in its proper place with the method of teaching by which students will acquire not merely a knowledge of those things to which the name of art is restricted by certain theorists, and will not only come to understand the laws of rhetoric, but will acquire that which will increase their powers of speech and nourish their eloquence. For as a rule the result of the dry textbooks on the art of rhetoric is that by straining after excessive subtlety they impair and cripple all the nobler elements of style, exhaust the life-blood of the imagination and leave but the bare bones, which, while it is right and necessary that they should exist and be bound each to each by their respective ligaments, require a covering of flesh as well.[7] I shall therefore avoid the precedent set by the majority and shall not restrict myself to this narrow conception of my theme, but shall include in my twelve books a brief demonstration of everything which may seem likely to contribute to the education of an orator. For if I were to attempt to say all that might be said on each subject, the book would never be finished.

26-27. Without natural gifts technical rules are useless. Similarly these gifts are of no profit in themselves without a skilful teacher, persistent study, continuous and extensive practice in writing, reading, and speaking.

There is however one point which I must emphasize before I begin, which is this. Without natural gifts technical rules are

---

7. So today, let teachers and writers of textbooks not kill their subjects by an unimaginative and routine presentation of the dry, dead bones of those subjects, necessary though the bones are; let them rather by an enthusiastic and humanistic treatment of those subjects put warm flesh on the bones and make them live. Cp. III.i.3-5 below and notes 1 and 2 thereon.

useless. Consequently the student who is devoid of talent will derive no more profit from this work than barren soil from a treatise on agriculture. There are, it is true, other natural aids, such as the possession of a good voice and robust lungs, sound health, powers of endurance and grace, and if these are possessed only to a moderate extent, they may be improved by methodical training. In some cases, however, these gifts are lacking to such an extent that their absence is fatal to all such advantages as talent and study can confer, while, similarly, they are of no profit in themselves unless cultivated by skilful teaching, persistent study and continuous and extensive practice in writing, reading and speaking.[8]

---

8. Skillful teachers, conscientious students, unrelenting practice in writing, reading, and speaking—aren't these still for us today among the leading essentials for success in education and in life despite the new-fangled jargons, theories, and devices? Jack Valenti, president of the Motion Picture Association of America, observed in the *Washington Post* of Sept. 11, 1971: "One widely prevalent notion today seems to demand instant achievement of goals, without any of the wearing, frustrating preparation that is indispensable to any task, . . . discipline of mind and spirit. . . .The horrifying truth becomes clear; there is no short cut, no magic carpet that sweeps them [young people] swiftly from desire to achievement."

BOOK I (CONTINUED)
CHAPTERS I—XII

(Elementary and Secondary Education)

Chapters i-iii. Preschool and Elementary Education

i.1-3. Most human beings are educable; and a father should be careful about the groundwork of his son's education. Most are quick to reason and ready to learn; and you do not find anyone who does not gain something from education.

I would, therefore, have a father conceive the highest hopes of his son from the moment of his birth. If he does so, he will be more careful about the groundwork of his education. For there is absolutely no foundation for the complaint that but few men have the power to take in the knowledge that is imparted to them, and that the majority are so slow of understanding that education is a waste of time and labour. On the contrary you will find that most are quick to reason and ready to learn. Reasoning comes as naturally to man as flying to birds, speed to horses and ferocity to beasts of prey: our minds are endowed by nature with such activity and sagacity that the soul is believed to proceed from heaven. Those who are dull and unteachable are as abnormal as prodigious births and monstrosities, and are but few in number. A proof of what I say is to be found in the fact that boys commonly show promise of many accomplishments, and when such promise dies away as they grow up, this is plainly due not to the failure of natural gifts, but to lack of the requisite care. But, it will be urged, there are degrees of talent. Undoubtedly, I reply, and there will be a corresponding variation in actual accomplishment: but that there are any who gain nothing from education, I absolutely deny.[1] The man who shares this conviction, must, as soon as he becomes a father, devote the utmost care to fostering the promise shown by the son whom he destines to become an orator.

i.4-11. Qualifications desirable in a nurse, parents, and a paedagogus; stress laid on as good an education as possible and on good character above all else; the importance of the family influence from the very beginning.

Above all see that the child's nurse speaks correctly. The ideal, according to Chrysippus,[2] would be that she should be a philosopher: failing that, he desired that the best should be chosen, as far as possible. No doubt the most important point is that they should be of good character:[3] but they should speak correctly as well. It is the nurse that the child first hears, and her words that he will first attempt to imitate. And we are by nature most tenacious of childish impressions, just as the flavour first absorbed by vessels when new persists, and the colour imparted by dyes to the primitive whiteness of wool is indelible. Further it is the worst impressions that are most durable. For, while what is good readily deteriorates, you will never turn vice into virtue. Do not therefore allow the boy to become accustomed even in infancy to a style of speech which he will subsequently have to unlearn.[4]

4

5

1. Starting with these two paragraphs in Quintilian, one thinks of Christopher Jencks' *Inequality, A Reassessment of the Effect of Family and Schooling in America* (Basic Books, Inc., Oct. 1972); but Jencks seems to be thinking primarily of the economic, the paycheck, potential and value of our present educational system. "All we are saying is that giving children better schools is not going to eliminate poverty and economic inequality among adults." He maintains that cognitive skill exercises little direct influence on job performance! On the other hand, he does admit that schooling is important and has great impact on people's lives. "Without schools few children would learn to read and virtually nobody would learn algebra." Obviously this topic is too big for any footnote, but it is bound to stir educational debate in the unending discussion about the educability of people and the objectives of education.

2. Chrysippus, a very famous Stoic philosopher of third century B.C.

3. Good character, or morality, is a recurrent theme emphasized throughout the entire work as a prime requirement for teachers and all others connected with students and as a prime element in education to be inculcated in students (e.g., I.ii.4-8; II.ii.1 and note 10 thereon, II.ii.14-15 below).

4. Cp. the whole defective situation and environment which necessitates headstart programs today and the question whether ghetto dialects and other uneducated English should be regarded as acceptable in comparison with the best standards of English usage. For far too many people seem to take almost irresponsible glee in mangling our English language; families and even schools in a lazy age of permissiveness are too often needlessly and reprehensibly lax in this matter.

(Elementary and Secondary Education) Bk. I.i

As regards parents, I should like to see them as highly educated 6
as possible, and I do not restrict this remark to fathers alone. We
are told that the eloquence of the Gracchi owed much to their
mother Cornelia, whose letters even today testify to the cultivation of her style. Laelia, the daughter of Gaius Laelius, is said to
have reproduced the elegance of her father's language in her own
speech, while the oration delivered before the triumvirs by Hortensia, the daughter of Quintus Hortensius, is still read and not
merely as a compliment to her sex. And even those who have not 7
had the fortune to receive a good education should not for that
reason devote less care to their son's education; but should on the
contrary show all the greater diligence in other matters where
they can be of service to their children.

As regards the boys in whose company our budding orator is to 8
be brought up, I would repeat what I have said about nurses. As
regards his *paedagogi*,[5] I would urge that they should have had a
thorough education, or if they have not, that they should be
aware of the fact. There are none worse than those, who as soon
as they have progressed beyond a knowledge of the alphabet
delude themselves into the belief that they are the possessors of
real knowledge.[6] For they disdain to stoop to the drudgery of
teaching, and conceiving that they have acquired a certain title to
authority—a frequent source of vanity in such persons—become
imperious or even brutal in instilling a thorough dose of their
own folly. Their misconduct is no less prejudicial to morals. We 9
are, for instance, told by Diogenes of Babylon, that Leonides,
Alexander's *paedagogus*, infected his pupil with certain faults,
which as a result of his education as a boy clung to him even in his
maturer years when he had become the greatest of kings.

If any of my readers regards me as somewhat exacting in my 10
demands, I would ask him to reflect that it is no easy task to create
an orator, even though his education be carried out under the
most favourable circumstances, and that further and greater

---

5. *Paedagogus*: derived from Greek *pais, paidos*, "boy, child," and *agogos*, "leader, guide, attendant"; the slave who escorted a boy to and from school and who watched over him in general. Although a paedagogus was not actually a schoolteacher, it is easy to see how our words "pedagogue" and "pedagogy" acquired their meaning, especially in view of the Greek *paideuein*, "to educate." Incidentally, be careful to note that the "ped-" in "ped-agogue" has nothing to do with Latin *pes, pedis*, "foot."

6. Apparently a *little* learning has always been a dangerous thing.

difficulties are still before us. For continuous application, the very best of teachers and a variety of exercises are necessary. Therefore the rules which we lay down for the education of our pupil must be of the best. If anyone refuses to be guided by them, the fault will lie not with the method, but with the individual. Still if it should prove impossible to secure the ideal nurse, the ideal companions, or the ideal *paedagogus,* I would insist that there should be one person at any rate attached to the boy who has some knowledge of speaking and who will, if any incorrect expression should be used by nurse or *paedagogus* in the presence of the child under their charge, at once correct the error and prevent its becoming a habit.[7] But it must be clearly understood that this is only a remedy, and that the ideal course is that indicated above.

i.12-14. Early and concurrent study of Greek and Latin; bilingualism of the Romans.

I prefer that a boy should begin with Greek, because Latin, being in general use, will be picked up by him whether we will or no; while the fact that Latin learning is derived from Greek is a further reason for his being first instructed in the latter. I do not however desire that this principle should be so superstitiously observed that he should for long speak and learn only Greek, as is done in the majority of cases. Such a course gives rise to many faults of language and accent; the latter tends to acquire a foreign intonation, while the former through force of habit becomes impregnated with Greeek idioms, which persist with extreme obstinacy even when we are speaking another tongue. The study of Latin ought therefore to follow at no great distance and in a short time proceed side by side with Greek.[8] The result will be that, as soon as we begin to give equal attention to both languages, neither will prove a hindrance to the other.

i.15-20. Should a child's education begin before the age of seven? Let us not waste the earliest years. However, in order that the young child may not be turned against his studies, let him be taught via amusement and encouraged by praise, competition, and rewards.

---

7. Note the necessity of immediate and constant correction of errors to avoid bad habits, certainly a practice equally valid for us today.

8. This bilingualism of the Romans provides a good example of the influence of Greek culture on Roman culture. Note that Cicero was thoroughly trained to orate in Greek as well as in Latin and highly valued the discipline received from his training in Greek.

(Elementary and Secondary Education)   Bk. I.i

Some hold that boys should not be taught to read till they are seven years old,[9] that being the earliest age at which they can derive profit from instruction and endure the strain of learning. Most of them attribute this view to Hesiod, at least such as lived before the time of Aristophanes the grammarian, who was the first to deny that the *Hypothecae,* in which this opinion is expressed, was the work of that poet. But other authorities, among them Eratosthenes, give the same advice. Those however who hold that a child's mind should not be allowed to lie fallow for a moment are wiser. Chrysippus, for instance, though he gives the nurses a three years' reign, still holds the formation of the child's mind on the best principles to be a part of their duties. Why, again, since children are capable of moral training, should they not be capable of literary education? I am well aware that during the whole period of which I am speaking we can expect scarcely the same amount of progress that one year will effect afterwards. Still those who disagree with me seem in taking this line to spare the teacher rather than the pupil. What better occupation can a child have so soon as he is able to speak? And he must be kept occupied somehow or other. Or why should we despise the profit to be derived before the age of seven, small though it be? For though the knowledge absorbed in the previous years may be but little, yet the boy will be learning something more advanced during that year, in which he would otherwise have been occupied with something more elementary. Such progress each successive year increases the total, and the time gained during childhood is clear profit to the period of youth. Further as regards the years which follow I must emphasise the importance of learning what has to be learnt in good time. Let us not therefore waste the earliest years: there is all the less excuse for this, since the elements of literary training are solely a question of memory, which not only exists even in small children, but is specially retentive at that age.

---

9. Similarly William Heard Kilpatrick in 1913 claimed that it was traumatic for children to learn to read before the second grade, i.e., before the age of seven. Thus he temporarily discredited Montessori and others who maintained that children could read at an earlier age and with enjoyment and profit. Now, however, the anti-intellectual "progressive" theories of Kilpatrick are being discredited and the pro-intellectual methods like Montessori's are being reinstated. (See Barr, pp. 290-291, 311.) Thus ancient educational debate has come full circle in modern educational debate, and we might as well have given heed to Quintilian's sound judgment in the first place.

I am not however so blind to differences of age as to think that the very young should be forced on prematurely or given real work to do. Above all things we must take care that the child, who is not old enough to love his studies, does not come to hate them and dread the bitterness which he has once tasted, even when the years of infancy are left behind. His studies must be made an amusement: he must be questioned and praised and taught to rejoice when he has done well; sometimes too, when he refuses instruction, it should be given to some other to excite his envy, at times also he must be engaged in competition and should be allowed to believe himself successful more often than not, while he should be encouraged to do his best by such rewards as may appeal to his tender years.

i.21-24. Such studies are not trivial in view of the child's infancy.

These instructions may seem but trivialities in view of the fact that I am professing to describe the education of an orator. But studies, like men, have their infancy, and as the training of the body which is destined to grow to the fulness of strength begins while the child is in his cradle and at his mother's breast, so even the man who is destined to rise to the heights of eloquence was once a squalling babe, tried to speak in stammering accents and was puzzled by the shapes of letters. Nor does the fact that capacity for learning is inadequate, prove that it is not necessary to learn anything. No one blames a father because he thinks that such details should on no account be neglected in the case of his own son. Why then should he be criticised who sets down for the benefit of the public what he would be right to put into practice in his own house? There is this further reason why he should not be blamed. Small children are better adapted for taking in small things, and just as the body can only be trained to certain flexions of the limbs while it is young and supple, so the acquisition of strength makes the mind offer greater resistance to the acquisition of most subjects of knowledge. Would Philip of Macedon have wished that his son Alexander should be taught the rudiments of letters by Aristotle, the greatest philosopher of that age, or would the latter have undertaken the task, if he had not thought that even the earliest instruction is best given by the most perfect teacher and has real reference to the whole of education? Let us assume therefore that Alexander has been confided to our charge and that the infant placed in our lap deserves no less

(Elementary and Secondary Education) Bk. I.i

attention than he—though for that matter every man's child deserves equal attention. Would you be ashamed even in teaching him the alphabet to point out some brief rules for his education?

i.24-29. On learning the shapes and names of the letters of the alphabet, and the art and desirability of writing them well, quickly, and legibly.

At any rate I am not satisfied with the course (which I note is usually adopted) of teaching small children the names and order of the letters before their shapes. Such a practice makes them slow to recognise the letters, since they do not pay attention to their actual shape, preferring to be guided by what they have already learned by rote. It is for this reason that teachers, when they think they have sufficiently familiarised their young pupils with the letters written in their usual order, reverse that order or rearrange it in every kind of combination, until they learn to know the letters from their appearance and not from the order in which they occur. It will be best therefore for children to begin by learning their appearance and names just as they do with men. The method, however, to which we have objected in teaching the alphabet, is unobjectionable when applied to syllables. I quite approve on the other hand of a practice which has been devised to stimulate children to learn by giving them ivory letters to play with, as I do of anything else that may be discovered to delight the very young, the sight, handling and naming of which is a pleasure.[10]

As soon as the child has begun to know the shapes of the various letters, it will be no bad thing to have them cut as accurately as possible upon a board, so that the pen[11] may be guided along the grooves. Thus mistakes such as occur with wax tablets will be rendered impossible; for the pen will be confined between the edges of the letters and will be prevented from going astray. Further by increasing the frequency and speed with which they follow these fixed outlines we shall give steadiness to the fingers, and there will be no need to guide the child's hand with our own. The art of writing well and quickly is not unimportant for our

---

10. This section makes one think of Montessori's didactic material and her emphasis on fun and games through sight, handling, and naming, then writing.

11. The Latin word here and throughout the passage is *stilus,* which means a hard-pointed instrument (more like our pencil than pen) used for writing on a wax-coated tablet.

purpose, though it is generally disregarded by persons of quality. Writing is of the utmost importance in the study which we have under consideration and by its means alone can true and deeply rooted proficiency be obtained. But a sluggish pen delays our thoughts, while an unformed and illiterate hand cannot be deciphered,[12] a circumstance which necessitates another wearisome task, namely the dictation of what we have written to a copyist. We shall therefore at all times and in all places, and above all when we are writing private letters to our friends, find a gratification in the thought that we have not neglected even this accomplishment.

i.30-31. Syllables, whatever the difficulty, must be thoroughly learned by repetition and memory; then words and sentences.

As regards syllables, no short cut is possible: they must all be learnt,[13] and there is no good in putting off learning the most difficult; this is the general practice, but the sole result is bad spelling. Further we must beware of placing a blind confidence in a child's memory. It is better to repeat[14] syllables and impress them on the memory and, when he is reading, not to press him to read continuously or with greater speed, unless indeed the clear and obvious sequence of letters can suggest itself without its being necessary for the child to stop to think. The syllables once learnt, let him begin to construct words with them and sentences with the words.

i.32-34. In learning to read, proceed slowly but surely; speed comes through practice.

You will hardly believe how much reading is delayed by undue

12. There is no virtue in a sloppy, illegible hand: it is no proof of intelligence and it exasperates all. Practically anybody, if he will take the trouble, can write clearly, though his hand need not be calligraphic. The script that one often sees on handwritten papers makes one feel that our grade schools are too commonly lax in this matter today and that they ought to heed Quintilian's advice—even though Roman "persons of quality" generally did not!

13. Anyone who has seen the disastrous results of the "whole-word recognition," "look-say," asyllabic method of learning how to read and has suffered with his children in trying to rectify this disaster by teaching them some phonics will wish that certain modern educationists had had the wisdom to resist their passion for innovation and had had the sense to follow the sane guidance of Quintilian in the first place. (See Barr, p. 279, and *Tomorrow's Illiterates: The State of Reading Instruction Today*, edited by Charles C. Walcutt for the Council of Basic Education.)

14. The old Latin saying *Repetitio mater memoriae* ("repetition is the mother of memory") is still valid and deserves to be preserved among educational devices.

haste.[15] If the child attempts more than his powers allow, the inevitable result is hesitation, interruption and repetition, and the mistakes which he makes merely lead him to lose confidence in what he already knows. Reading must therefore first be sure, then connected, while it must be kept slow for a considerable time, until practice brings speed unaccompanied by error. For to look to the right, which is regularly taught, and to look ahead depends not so much on precept as on practice; since it is necessary to keep the eyes on what follows while reading out what precedes, with the resulting difficulty that the attention of the mind must be divided, the eyes and voice being differently engaged.

i.34-37. Writing should be practiced via the less common words and also moral aphorisms and lines of poetry, which can then from the earliest beginning be memorized for the training of both character and memory. The importance of memory training by practice. The value of tongue twisters in the disciplining of pronunciation.

It will be found worth while, when the boy begins to write out words in accordance with the usual practice, to see that he does not waste his labour in writing out common words of everyday occurrence. He can readily learn the explanations or glosses, as the Greeks call them, of the more obscure words by the way and, while he is still engaged on the first rudiments, acquire what would otherwise demand special time to be devoted to it. And as we are still discussing minor details, I would urge that the lines, which he is set to copy, should not express thoughts of no significance, but convey some sound moral lesson. He will remember such aphorisms even when he is an old man, and the impression made upon his unformed mind will contribute to the formation of his character. He may also be entertained by learning the sayings of famous men and above all selections from the poets, poetry being more attractive to children. For memory is most necessary to an orator, as I shall point out in its proper place, and there is nothing like practice for strengthening and developing it. And at the tender age of which we are now speaking, when originality is impossible, memory is almost the only faculty which

---

15. *Festina lente* ("make haste slowly"), said Emperor Augustus: take care and time to lay good, reliable foundations, for without them any precipitate rush to quick, showy, unsubstantial effects will prove futile and a waste of time. Cp. notes 3 and 8 in Preface above and 36 below; also I.iv.22; II,iv.17; X.iii,5,8-10.

can be developed by the teacher. It will be worth while, by way of improving the child's pronunciation and distinctness of utterance, to make him rattle off a selection of names and lines of studied difficulty: they should be formed of a number of syllables which go ill together and should be harsh and rugged in sound: the Greeks call them "gags." This sounds a trifling matter, but its omission will result in numerous faults of pronunciation, which, unless removed in early years, will become a perverse and incurable habit and persist through life.

ii.1-3. The boy reaches the age of formal education. The controversy over whether it is better for him to be educated at home by a private tutor or to be placed in a "public" school involves two considerations: (1) morality; (2) academic attention.

But the time has come for the boy to grow up little by little, to leave the nursery and tackle his studies in good earnest. This therefore is the place to discuss the question as to whether it is better to have him educated privately at home or hand him over to some large school and those whom I may call public instructors.[16] The latter course has, I know, won the approval of most eminent authorities and of those who have formed the national character of the most famous states. It would, however, be folly to shut our eyes to the fact that there are some who disagree with this preference for public education owing to a certain prejudice in favour of private tuition. These persons seem to be guided in the main by two principles. In the interests of morality they would avoid the society of a number of human beings at an age that is specially liable to acquire serious faults: I only wish I could deny the truth of the view that such education has often been the cause of the most discreditable actions. Secondly they hold that whoever is to be the boy's teacher, he will devote his time more generously to one pupil than if he has to divide it among several. The first reason certainly deserves serious consideration. If it were proved that schools, while advantageous to study, are prejudicial to morality, I should give my vote for virtuous living in preference to even supreme excellence of speaking. But in my opinion the two are inseparable. I hold that no one can be a true orator unless he is also a good man and, even

---

16. "Public" in the sense that they are available to all who would pay the tuition fees, as in our private schools today; the Roman "public" schools were not free schools supported by tax money and run by the state.

(Elementary and Secondary Education) Bk. I.ii

if he could be, I would not have it so. I will therefore deal with this point first.

ii.4-8. Actually morals may be corrupted at home as well as at school, depending on the integrity of the people involved. In this the responsibility of the parents is very great; their failure is far too often horrendous. "Would that we did not too often ruin our children's character ourselves!" A terrific indictment of the older generation.

It is held that schools corrupt the morals. It is true that this is sometimes the case. But morals may be corrupted at home as well. There are numerous instances of both, as there are also of the preservation of a good reputation under either circumstance. The nature of the individual boy and the care devoted to his education make all the difference. Given a natural bent toward evil or negligence in developing and watching over modest behaviour in early years, privacy will provide equal opportunity for sin. The teacher employed at home may be of bad character, and there is just as much danger in associating with bad slaves as there is with immodest companions of good birth. On the other hand if the natural bent be towards virtue, and parents are not afflicted with a blind and torpid indifference,[17] it is possible to choose a teacher of the highest character (and those who are wise will make this their first object), to adopt a method of education of the strictest kind and at the same time to attach some respectable man or faithful freedman to their son as his friend and guardian, that his unfailing companionship may improve the character even of those who gave rise to apprehension.

Yet how easy were the remedy for such fears. Would that we did not too often ruin our children's character ourselves! We spoil

17. Quintilian once more throughout §§4-8 emphasizes the importance and the responsibilities of the parents and their example. Very sad to say, we again today, amid affluence and laxity akin to that of imperial Rome, find this "blind and torpid indifference" among too many parents in the fact that they not only fail to back up a teacher's attempts to administer reasonable discipline according to the laws of the institution but almost seem to encourage their children to defy and ridicule the school authorities. The obvious and ugly result in our public schools, at any rate, is that many teachers, living in terror of the anarchistic *enfants terribles* and the irresponsible and sometimes delinquent parents, fear for their positions, if not their lives, and are helpless to excercise that reasonable control over their students which the students truly need and, as a rule, subconsciously desire. Is this the awful heritage of overindulgent permissiveness, "progressive" education and excessively child-centered education? Need these excesses continue? Oh for the Graeco-Roman ideal of the golden mean between extremes!

them from the cradle. That soft upbringing, which we call kindness, saps all the sinews both of mind and body. If the child crawls on purple, what will he not desire when he comes to manhood? Before he can talk he can distinguish scarlet and cries for the very best brand of purple. We train their palates before we teach their lips to speak. They grow up in litters:[18] if they set foot to earth, they are supported by the hands of attendants on either side. We rejoice if they say something over-free, and words which we should not tolerate from the lips even of an Alexandrian page are greeted with laughter and a kiss. We have no right to be surprised. It was we that taught them: they hear us use such words, they see our mistresses and minions; every dinner party is loud with foul songs, and things are presented to their eyes of which we should blush to speak. Hence springs habit, and habit in time becomes second nature. The poor children learn these things before they know them to be wrong. They become luxurious and effeminate, and far from acquiring such vices at schools, introduce them themselves.

ii.9-16. Academically more benefits are likely to accrue from teachers in the school than from private tutors in the home. Homework, lectures, concern of a good teacher, special attention.

I now turn to the objection that one master can give more attention to one pupil. In the first place there is nothing to prevent the principle of "one teacher, one boy" being combined with school education. And even if such a combination should prove impossible, I should still prefer the broad daylight of a respectable school to the solitude and obscurity of a private education. For all the best teachers pride themselves on having a large number of pupils and think themselves worthy of a bigger audience. On the other hand in the case of inferior teachers a consciousness of their own defects not seldom reconciles them to being attached to a single pupil and playing the part—for it amounts to little more—of a mere *paedagogus*.

But let us assume that influence, money or friendship succeed in securing a paragon of learning to teach the boy at home. Will he be able to devote the whole day to one pupil? Or can we demand such continuous attention on the part of the learner? The mind is as easily tired as the eye, if given no relaxation.

---

18. Litter: a curtained couch or bed carried on poles by slaves. It might be thought of as roughly equivalent to our automobile.

(Elementary and Secondary Education) Bk. I.ii

Moreover by far the larger proportion of the learner's time ought to be devoted to private study. The teacher does not stand over him while he is writing or thinking or learning by heart. While he is so occupied the intervention of anyone, be he who he may, is a hindrance. Further, not all reading requires to be first read aloud or interpreted by a master. If it did, how would the boy ever become acquainted with all the authors required of him? A small time only is required to give purpose and direction to the day's work, and consequently individual instruction can be given to more than one pupil. There are moreover a large number of subjects in which it is desirable that instruction should be given to all the pupils simultaneously. I say nothing of the analyses and declamations of the professors of rhetoric: in such cases there is no limit to the number of the audience, as each individual pupil will in any case receive full value. The voice of a lecturer is not like a dinner which will only suffice for a limited number; it is like the sun which distributes the same quantity of light and heat to all of us. So too with the teacher of literature. Whether he speak of style or expound disputed passages, explain stories or paraphrase poems, everyone who hears him will profit by his teaching. But, it will be urged, a large class is unsuitable for the correction of faults or for explanation. It may be inconvenient; one cannot hope for absolute perfection; but I shall shortly contrast the inconvenience with the obvious advantages.

Still I do not wish a boy to be sent where he will be neglected. But a good teacher will not burden himself with a larger number of pupils than he can manage, and it is further of the very first importance that he should be on friendly and intimate terms with us and make his teaching not a duty but a labour of love.[19] Then there will never be any question of being swamped by the number of our fellow-learners. Moreover any teacher who has the least tincture of literary culture will devote special attention to any boy who shows signs of industry and talent; for such a pupil will redound to his own credit. But even if large schools are to be avoided, a proposition from which I must dissent if the size be due to the excellence of the teacher, it does not follow that all schools

---

19. "Not a duty but a labor of love." Actually nobody should go into teaching merely because of the paycheck, for in that case teaching will be nothing but a routine job; ideally a person should enter teaching only if he feels called to it by his love for his subject and for people, in which case teaching will be an inspiring vocation (a calling).

are to be avoided. It is one thing to avoid them, another to select the best.

ii.17-31. Great advantages derive from the public, common, social experience at a school: comparison with others, learning from their merits and faults, friendships, the value of competition inter pares *and of commendation, the fact that a teacher exerts himself to the full more for a group of students than for a solitary student.*

Having refuted these objections, let me now explain my own views. It is above all things necessary that our future orator, who willl have to live in the utmost publicity and in the broad daylight of public life, should become accustomed from his childhood to move in society without fear and habituated to a life far removed from that of the pale student, the solitary and recluse. His mind requires constant stimulus and excitement, whereas retirement such as has just been mentioned induces languor and the mind becomes mildewed like things that are left in the dark, or else flies to the opposite extreme and becomes puffed up with empty conceit; for he who has no standard of comparison by which to judge his own powers will necessarily rate them too high. Again when the fruits of his study have to be displayed to the public gaze, our recluse is blinded by the sun's glare, and finds everything new and unfamiliar, for though he has learnt what is required to be done in public, his learning is but the theory of a hermit. I say nothing of friendships which endure unbroken to old age having acquired the binding force of a sacred duty: for initiation in the same studies has all the sanctity of initiation in the same mysteries of religion. And where shall he acquire that instinct which we call common feeling, if he secludes himself from that intercourse which is natural not merely to mankind but even to dumb animals? Further, at home he can only learn what is taught to himself, while at school he will learn what is taught others as well. He will hear many merits praised and many faults corrected every day: he will derive equal profit from hearing the indolence of a comrade rebuked or his industry commended. Such praise will incite him to emulation, he will think it a disgrace to be outdone by his contemporaries and a distinction to surpass his seniors. All such incentives provide a valuable stimulus, and though ambition may be a fault in itself, it is often the mother of virtues.

I remember that my own masters had a practice which was not

without advantages. Having distributed the boys in classes, they made the order in which they were to speak depend on their ability, so that the boy who had made most progress in his studies had the privilege of declaiming first. The performances on these occasions were criticised. To win commendation was a tremendous honour, but the prize most eagerly coveted was to be the leader of the class. Such a position was not permanent. Once a month the defeated competitors were given a fresh opportunity of competing for the prize. Consequently success did not lead the victor to relax his efforts, while the vexation caused by defeat served as an incentive to wipe out the disgrace. I will venture to assert that to the best of my memory this practice did more to kindle our oratorical ambitions than all the exhortations of our instructors, the watchfulness of our *paedagogi* and the prayers of our parents.

Further while emulation promotes progress in the more advanced pupils, beginners who are still of tender years derive greater pleasure from imitating their comrades than their masters, just because it is easier. For children still in the elementary stages of education can scarce dare hope to reach that complete eloquence which they understand to be their goal: their ambition will not soar so high, but they will imitate the vine which has to grasp the lower branches of the tree on which it is trained before it can reach the topmost boughs. So true is this that it is the master's duty as well, if he is engaged on the task of training unformed minds and prefers practical utility to a more ambitious programme, not to burden his pupils at once with tasks to which their strength is unequal, but to curb his energies and refrain from talking over the heads of his audience. Vessels with narrow mouths will not receive liquids if too much be poured into them at a time, but are easily filled if the liquid is admitted in a gentle stream or, it may be, drop by drop; similarly you must consider how much a child's mind is capable of receiving: the things which are beyond their grasp will not enter their minds, which have not opened out sufficiently to take them in. It is a good thing therefore that a boy should have companions whom he will desire first to imitate and then to surpass: thus he will be led to aspire to higher achievement.

I would add that the instructors themselves cannot develop the same intelligence and energy before a single listener as they can when inspired by the presence of a numerous audience. For eloquence depends in the main on the state of the mind, which must be moved, conceive images and adapt itself to suit the nature of the subject which is the theme of speech. Further the loftier and the more elevated the mind, the more powerful will be the forces which move it: consequently praise gives it growth and effort increase, and the thought that it is doing something great fills it with joy. The duty of stooping to expend that power of speaking which has been acquired at the cost of such effort upon an audience of one gives rise to a silent feeling of disdain, and the teacher is ashamed to raise his voice above the ordinary conversational level. Imagine the air of a declaimer, or the voice of an orator, his gait, his delivery, the movements of his body, the emotions of his mind, and, to go no further, the fatigue of his exertions, all for the sake of one listener! Would he not seem little less than a lunatic? No, there would be no such thing as eloquence, if we spoke only with one person at a time.

iii. On the capacity and treatment of pupils.

iii.1-5. The skillful teacher sizes up the nature and capacity of his pupils: memory, power of imitation, character, ostentatious precocity.

The skilful teacher will make it his first care, as soon as a boy is entrusted to him, to ascertain his ability and character. The surest indication in a child is his power of memory. The characteristics of a good memory are twofold: it must be quick to take in and faithful to retain impressions of what it receives. The indication of next importance is the power of imitation: for this is a sign that the child is teachable: but he must imitate merely what he is taught, and must not, for example, mimic someone's gait or bearing or defects. For I have no hope that a child will turn out well who loves imitation merely for the purpose of raising a laugh. He who is really gifted will also above all else be good. For the rest, I regard slowness of intellect as preferable to actual badness. But a good boy will be quite unlike the dullard and the sloth. My ideal pupil will absorb instruction with ease and will even ask some questions; but he will follow rather than anticipate his teacher. Precocious intellects rarely produce sound fruit. By the precocious I mean those who perform small tasks with ease and, thus emboldened, proceed to display all their little accomplishments without being asked; but their accomplishments are only of the most obvious kind: they string words together and trot them out

(Elementary and Secondary Education) Bk. I.ii, iii

boldly and undeterred by the slightest sense of modesty. Their actual achievement is small, but what they can do they perform with ease. They have no real power and what they have is but of shallow growth: it is as when we cast seed on the surface of the soil: it springs up too rapidly, the blade apes the loaded ear, and yellows ere harvest time, but bears no grain. Such tricks please us when we contrast them with the performer's age, but progress soon stops and our admiration withers away.

iii.6-7. The teacher must consider how to treat the different pupils according to their temperaments; the ideal pupil.

Such indications once noted, the teacher must next consider what treatment is to be applied to the mind of his pupil. There are some boys who are slack, unless pressed on: others again are impatient of control: some are amenable to fear, while others are paralysed by it: in some cases the mind requires continued application to form it, in others this result is best obtained by rapid concentration. Give me the boy who is spurred on by praise, delighted by success and ready to weep over failure. Such an one must be encouraged by appeals to his ambition; rebuke will bite him to the quick; honour will be a spur, and there is no fear of his proving indolent.

iii.8-13. Reasonable relaxation and play are necessary; games reveal character and can thus help to mould it.

Still, all our pupils will require some relaxation, not merely because there is nothing in this world that can stand continued strain and even unthinking and inanimate objects are unable to maintain their strength, unless given intervals of rest, but because study depends on the good will of the student,[20] a quality that cannot be secured by compulsion. Consequently if restored and refreshed by a holiday, they will bring greater energy to their learning and approach their work with greater spirit of a kind that will not submit to be driven. I approve of play in the young; it is a sign of a lively disposition; nor will you ever lead me to believe that a boy who is gloomy and in a continual state of depression is

---

20. A most important point so often not grasped by inexperienced teachers nor by unfeeling educational martinets. A teacher should strive to win the co-operation of his pupils by persuasion (i.e., by making the activity seem "very sweet" [Latin *per-suavis*], attractive, relevant) and by explanation to make clear why this or that work to be done by the pupil is advantageous to him. Cp. what Quintilian says about flogging in §§ 13-18 below.

ever likely to show alertness of mind in his work, lacking as he does the impulse most natural to boys of his age. Such relaxation must not however be unlimited: otherwise the refusal to give a holiday will make boys hate their work, while excessive indulgence will accustom them to idleness. There are moreover certain games which have an educational value for boys, as for instance when they compete in posing each other with all kinds of questions which they ask turn and turn about. Games too reveal character in the most natural way, at least that is so if the teacher will bear in mind that there is no child so young as to be unable to learn to distinguish between right and wrong, and that the character is best moulded, when it is still guiltless of deceit and most susceptible to instruction: for once a bad habit has become engrained, it is easier to break than bend. There must be no delay, then, in warning a boy that his actions must be unselfish, honest, self-controlled, and we must never forget the words of Virgil,

"So strong is custom formed in early years."

iii.13-18. Punishment: arguments against the custom of flogging pupils and the abuses perpetrated by unprincipled teachers.

I disapprove of flogging,[21] although it is the regular custom and meets with the acquiescence of Chrysippus, because in the first place it is a disgraceful form of punishment and fit only for slaves, and is in any case an insult, as you will realize if you imagine its infliction at a later age. Secondly if a boy is so insensible to instruction that reproof is useless, he will, like the worst type of slave, merely become hardened to blows. Finally there will be absolutely no need of such punishment if the master is a thorough disciplinarian. As it is, we try to make amends for the negligence of the boy's *paedagogus,* not by forcing him to do what is right, but by punishing him for not doing what is right. And though you may compel a child with blows, what are you to do with him when he is a young man no longer amenable to such threats and confronted with tasks of far greater difficulty? Moreover when children are beaten, pain or fear frequently have results of which

21. Quintilian is justly famous for his humanity at a time when severe corporal punishment was the rule. This educational problem has continued down to our own times and is still with us, being currently debated within the National Education Association, for example.

(Elementary and Secondary Education) Bk. I.iii, iv

it is not pleasant to speak and which are likely subsequently to be a source of shame, a shame which unnerves and depresses the mind and leads the child to shun and loathe the light. Further if inadequate care is taken in the choices of respectable governors and instructors, I blush to mention the shameful abuse which scoundrels sometimes make of their right to administer corporal punishment or the opportunity not infrequently offered to others by the fear thus caused in the victims. I will not linger on this subject; it is more than enough if I have made my meaning clear. I will content myself with saying that children are helpless and easily victimised, and that therefore no one should be given unlimited power over them. I will now proceed to describe the subjects in which the boy must be trained, if he is to become an orator, and to indicate the age at which each should be commenced.

Chapters iv-xii. After his elementary education under the litterator[22] *(see Chapters i-iii above), the student now enters on his course of secondary education under the* grammaticus.[23]

iv.1-5. The grammaticus *teaches both Greek and Latin languages and literatures: the art of speaking and writing correctly and the interpretation of the poets. In fact, all kinds of writings are to be read for their subject matter and vocabulary, including music, astronomy, and philosophy. Literature is the cornerstone of a liberal education and is a constant delight throughout life.*

As soon as the boy has learned to read and write[24] without difficulty, it is the turn for the teacher of literature. My words apply equally to Greek and Latin masters, though I prefer that a start should be made with a Greek:[25] in either case the method is the same. This profession may be most briefly considered under two heads, the art of speaking correctly and the interpretation of

---

22. *Litterator*: elementary school teacher of writing (Latin *littera, a letter of the alphabet*), syllables, reading and the like.

23. *Grammaticus* derives from Greek *graphein*, "to write," but is a word of broad meaning in Latin. It covers not only the various aspects of language study (including, of course, grammar in our sense of the word, and writing and speaking correctly) but also the study of literature.

24. "To read and write": in Quintilian's Latin text the order is "to write and read," correctly corresponding with the order of learning (writing, syllables, reading) which he gave above in I.i.24-34.

25. Again note the bilingualism of the educated Roman. Cp. I.i.12-14 and note 8 above.

the poets; but there is more beneath the surface than meets the eye. For the art of writing is combined with that of speaking, and correct reading precedes interpretation, while in each of these cases criticism has its work to perform. Nor is it sufficient to have read the poets only: every kind of writer must be carefully studied, nor merely for the subject matter, but for the vocabulary; for words often acquire authority from their use by a particular author. Nor can such training be regarded as complete if it stop short of music, for the teacher of literature has to speak of metre and rhythm: nor again if he be ignorant of astronomy, can he understand the poets; for they, to mention no further points, frequently give their indications of time by reference to the rising and setting of the stars. Ignorance of philosophy is an equal drawback, since there are numerous passages in almost every poem based on the most intricate questions of natural philosophy,[26] while among the Greeks we have Empedocles and among our own poets Varro and Lucretius, all of whom have expounded their philosophies in verse. No small powers of eloquence also are required to enable the teacher to speak appropriately and fluently on the various points which have just been mentioned.[27] For this reason those who criticise the art of teaching literature as trivial and lacking in substance put themselves out of court. Unless the foundations of oratory are well and truly laid by the teaching of literature, the superstructure will collapse. The study of literature is a necessity for boys and the delight of old age, the sweet companion of our privacy and the sole branch of study which has more solid substance than display.[28]

26. Note that at this stage Quintilian refers to *natural* philosophy dealing with the world of nature and her laws in contrast to abstract theoretical moral philosophy, which for the most part comes later. For example, in his *De Natura Rerum* Lucretius expounded a Greek atomic theory to explain the nature of the universe scientifically.

27. Let the education student carefully add up the extent of the knowledge and eloquence required of a teacher "to enable the teacher to speak appropriately and fluently on the various points which have just been mentioned"; and let her or him be advised that the art of teaching literature—or any other subject for that matter—is nothing trivial. For it is not enough to have merely educational theory and know-how; one must far more importantly have a broad and accurate knowledge of the substance of one's subject.

28. Be it noted that literature is not only the foundation of successful oratory, but it is an essential element in the education and life of all people whether in school or afterwards. Said Cicero in *Pro Archia*, vii.16: "These studies [i.e., literature] nourish youth, entertain old age, add embellishment to our prosperity, provide refuge and solace in adversity, they give us delight at home, they are no hindrance when we are away from home, they watch through the night with us, they travel abroad with us, they attend us in our rustication."

(Elementary and Secondary Education) Bk. I.iv

iv.6-9,17-20,22. A few typical examples of Latin linguistics which a grammaticus should be prepared to teach his students: pronunciation, interesting matters about the alphabet, syllables, parts of speech, declensions and conjugations. (Quintilian's text here contains a vast amount of material not readily understandable by the Latinless reader.)

The elementary stages of the teaching of literature must not therefore be despised as trivial. It is of course an easy task to point out the difference between vowels and consonants, and to subdivide the latter into semi-vowels and mutes. But as the pupil gradually approaches the inner shrine of the sacred place, he will come to realize the intricacy of the subject, an intricacy calculated not merely to sharpen the wits of a boy, but to exercise even the most profound knowledge and erudition. It is not every ear that can appreciate the correct sound of the different letters. It is fully as hard as to distinguish the different notes in music. But all teachers of literature will condescend to such minutiae: they will discuss for instance whether certain necessary letters are absent from the alphabet, not indeed when we are writing Greek words (for then we borrow two letters[29] from them), but in the case of genuine Latin words: for example in words such as *seruus* and *uulgus* we feel the lack of the Aeolic digamma.[30] Again there is the question whether certain letters are not superfluous: for instance *k*,[31] which is also used as an abbreviation for certain nouns, and there is also *x*, the last letter of our own alphabet, which we could dispense with.[32]

The next subject to which attention must be given is that of syllables, of which I will speak briefly, when I come to deal with orthography.

Following this the teacher concerned will note the number and nature of the parts of speech, although there is some dispute as to their number. Earlier writers, among them Aristotle himself and Theodectes, hold that there are but three, *verbs, nouns,* and

29. The letters Y and Z were borrowed from the Greek alphabet in spelling Greek words taken over into Latin, and English inherited these letters from Latin—e.g., in *zephyrus, zodiacus*. (Incidentally, the so-called Roman alphabet is actually a form of the Greek alphabet.)

30. Digamma, a letter with the sound of our *w* (early lost from the Greek alphabet). In most modern Latin texts it is represented by *v* (the pointed form of *u*) with the ancient Roman sound of our *w*: *servus, vulgus*.

31. Since *c* in ancient Latin was always hard, *k* was unnecessary but was arbitrarily preserved in such words as *Kalendae* (our calendar) and Kathargo (our Carthage).

32. Since the compound consonant *x* = *ks* or Latin *cs*, the letter *x* was actually unnecessary, as it is with us; e.g., *ex* (from) = *ecs. sex* (six) = *secs.*

convinctions. Their view was that the force of language resided in the verbs, and the matter in the nouns (for the one is what we speak, the other that which we speak about), while the duty of the convinctions was to provide a link between the nouns and the verbs. I know the *conjunction* is the term in general use. But *convinction*[33] seems to me to be the more accurate translation of the Greek *syndesmos.* Gradually the number was increased by the philosophers, more especially by the Stoics: *articles* were first added to the convinctions, then *prepositions*: to nouns *appellations*[34] were added, then the *pronoun* and finally the *participle,* which holds a middle position between the verb and the noun. To the verb itself was added the *adverb.* Our own language dispenses with the articles, which are therefore distributed among the other parts of speech. But *interjections* must be added to those already mentioned.

Boys should begin by learning to decline nouns and conjugate verbs:[35] otherwise they will never be able to understand the next subject of study. This admonition would be superfluous but for the fact that most teachers, misled by a desire to show rapid progress, begin with what should really come at the end: their passion for displaying their pupils' talents in connexion with the more imposing aspects of their work serves but to delay progress and their short cut to knowledge merely lengthens the journey.[36]

33. Convinction (from *con,* "together," + *vincio,* "bind"), that which binds together, a conjunction; *syndesmos* (*syn,* "together," + *deo,* "bind").

34. "Appellations" were a special kind of intangible, not concrete, nouns like *wind, heaven, virtue.*

35. Those who have studied Latin may be amazed to read that ancient Roman boys, after having learned to speak and read Latin by the natural, direct method in their own families, among their friends, and in the elementary school, are now years later at the beginning of their secondary school education told by the greatest Latin teacher that they must at this point study declensions and conjugations to achieve greater accuracy and excellence. This corroborates the validity of our insistence on courses which provide a better understanding of our own English language and its usage, vocabulary, diction, and style. One also is, perhaps superficially, reminded of the current debate among Latin teachers between on the one hand the traditionalists, who believe in a thorough study of Latin forms and syntax accompanied by an analysis of the thoughts and experiences of the ancient Romans, and on the other hand the natural methodists, who claim that by dint of structured repetition they can quickly get students to speak and read Latin with little conscious formal study of inflections and syntax. The history of education is full of such conflicts; only time, the great sifter, and suffering will tell, as for instance in the case of "progressive education."

36. Again Quintilian cries out against shoddy shortcuts to showy ephemeral effects, which have no firm and lasting foundations. Cp. I.iii.3-5 and note 15 above, *et passim.*

(Elementary and Secondary Education)   Bk. I.iv, v

v.1. Language has three kinds of excellence: correctness, lucidity, and elegance. The teacher must observe the rules of correctness.

Style[37] has three kinds of excellence; correctness, lucidity, and elegance (for many include the all-important quality of appropriateness under the heading of elegance). Its faults are likewise threefold, namely the opposites of these excellences. The teacher of literature therefore must study the rules for correctness of speech, these constituting the first part of his art.

v.5-13. Barbarisms and solecisms must not be permitted. It is the duty of teachers to set an example of correctness for their pupils. (Cp. Chaucer's "If gold rust, what will iron do?") Barbarisms discussed.

In the first place barbarisms and solecisms must not be allowed to intrude their offensive presence. These blemishes are however pardoned at times, because we have become accustomed to them or because they have age or authority in their favour or are near akin to positive excellences, since it is often difficult to distinguish such blemishes from figures of speech. The teacher therefore, that such slippery customers may not elude detection, must seek to acquire delicate discrimination: but of this I will speak later when I come to discuss figures of speech. For the present I will define *barbarism* as an offense occurring in connexion with single works. Some of my readers may object that such a topic is beneath the dignity of so ambitious a work. But who does not know that some barbarisms occur in writing, others in speaking? For although what is incorrect in writing will also be incorrect in speech, the converse is not necessarily true, inasmuch as mistakes in writing are caused by addition or omission, substitution or transposition, while mistakes in speaking are due to separation or combination of syllables, to aspiration or other errors of sound. Trivial as these points may seem, our boys are still at school and I am reminding their instructors of their duty.[38] And if one of our teachers is lacking in education and has done no more than set foot in the outer courts of his art, he will have to confine himself to the rules published in the elementary text-books: the more learned teacher on the other hand will be in a position to go much further: first of all, for example, he will point out that there are many different kinds of barbarism. One kind is due to race, such

---

37. Style, i.e., language, speech *(oratio* is the word in the Latin text).

38. It would almost go without saying that it is the duty of teachers to correct students' barbarisms and solecisms were it not that then apparently, as now, some teachers could be lax or limited enough to let such errors pass undetected and uncorrected—which, of course, is no kindness to the student.

as the insertion of a Spanish or African term; for instance the iron tire of a wheel is called *cantus,* though Persius uses it as established in the Latin language; Catullus picked up *ploxenum* (a box) in the valley of the Po, while the author of the *in Pollionem,* be he Labienus or Cornelius Gallus, imported *casamo* from Gaul in the sense of "follower." As for *mastruca,* which is Sardinian for a "rough coat," it is introduced by Cicero merely as an object of derision. Another kind of barbarism proceeds from the speaker's temper: for instance, we regard it as barbarous if a speaker use cruel or brutal language. A third and very common kind, of which anyone may fashion examples for himself, consists in the addition or omission of a letter or syllable, or in the substitution of one for another or in placing one where it has no right to be. Some teachers however, to display their learning, are in the habit of picking out examples of *barbarism* from the poets and attacking the authors whom they are expounding for using such words. A boy should however realize that in poets such peculiarities are pardonable or even praiseworthy, and should therefore be taught less common instances. For Tinga of Placentia, if we may believe Hortensius who takes him to task for it, committed two *barbarisms* in one word by saying *precula* for *pergula:* that is to say he substituted *c* for *g,* and transposed *r* and *e.* Substitution is however sometimes admitted even in prose, as for instance when Cicero speaks of the army of *Canopus* which is locally styled *Canobus,* while the number of authors who have been guilty of transposition in writing *Trasumennus* for *Tarsumennus* has succeeded in standardising the error.

v.34,36-38,54. A solecism (a substandard or ungrammatical usage) involves more words than one or it may occur in a solitary word where another word is understood with it. Finally Quintilian's concluding statement after further discussion meaningless to the reader who knows no Latin.

All other faults in speaking are concerned with more words that one; among this class of faults is the *solecism,* although there have been controversies about this as well. Those who raise the question as to whether a *solecism* can arise in a single word show greater intelligence. Is it for instance a *solecism* if a man when calling a single person to him says *venite,* or dismissing several

(Elementary and Secondary Education) Bk. I.v

persons says *abi* or *discede*?[39] Or again if the answer does not correspond to the question: suppose, for example, when someone said to you "Whom do I see?", you were to reply "I."[40] Some too think it a *solecism* if the spoken word is contradicted by the motion of hand or head. I do not entirely concur with this view nor yet do I wholly dissent. I admit that a *solecism* may occur in a single word, but with this proviso: there must be something else equivalent to another word, to which the word, in which the error lies, can be referred, so that the *solecism* arises from the faulty connexion of those symbols by which facts are expressed and purpose indicated. To avoid all suspicion of quibbling, I will say that a *solecism* may occur in one word, but never in a word in isolation. I have said enough about *solecisms;* for I did not set out to write a treatise on grammar, but was unwilling to slight the science by passing it by without salutation, when it met me in the course of my journey.

v.55-58,71-72. Words proper, foreign, metaphorical, and newly coined.

I therefore resume the path which I prescribed for myself and point out that words are either native or foreign. Foreign words, like our population and our institutions, have come to us from practically every nation upon earth. I pass by words of Tuscan,

---

39. *Venite* is imperative *plural* as in *Venite, adoremus,* "Come *ye,* let us adore." The *singular* is *veni,* "come *thou.*" Similarly *abi* and *discede* are *singular,* both meaning "depart thou." The *plural* is *abite, discedite,* "depart ye." The illustration, perfectly clear in Latin, is not quite so clear in English because we use the same form for the imperative singular and plural and almost never use the singular or plural pronoun subject outside of older religious or poetic language as in "Come thou, almighty King," or "Seek ye first the Kingdom of Heaven."

40. Since pronouns are among the few words in English which still retain their old inflected forms, the Latin solecism (substandard or incorrect grammatical usage) here can be exactly reproduced. For the reply to the question "Whom do I see?" should be "Me"; i.e., "you see me." The solecism could have been compounded by phrasing the question "Who do I see?" Incidentally, the word "solecism" derives from Soloi, a city in Asia Minor whose citizens spoke Greek carelessly and incorrectly. With regard to solecisms and similar matters teachers should be very demanding of themselves as well as of their students—more demanding than many commonly are. All teachers and all students, whatever their subjects and courses, should undergo unflagging discipline (training) in accurate and effective language. For is not language one of the very greatest tools which *homo sapiens* possesses? Jive and gobbledegook will, we believe, prove to be ephemeral.

Sabine and Praenestine origin; for though Lucilius attacks Vettius for using them, and Pollio reproves Livy for his lapses into the dialect of Padua, I may be allowed to regard all such words as of native origin. Many Gallic words have become current coin, such as *raeda* (chariot) and *petorritum* (four-wheeled wagon) of which Cicero uses the former and Horace the latter. *Mappa* (napkin)[41] again, a word familiar in connexion with the circus, is claimed by the Carthaginians, while I have heard that *gurdus,* which is colloquially used in the sense of "stupid," is derived from Spain. But this distinction between native and foreign words has reference chiefly to Greek. For Latin is largely derived[42] from that language, and we use words which are admittedly Greek to express things for which we have no Latin equivalent. Similarly they at times borrow words from us.

Words are *proper* when they bear their original meaning; *metaphorical,* when they are used in a sense different from their natural meaning. *Current* words are safest to use: there is a spice of danger in coining *new.* For if they are adopted, our style wins but small glory from them; while if they are rejected, they become a subject for jest. Still we must make the venture; for as Cicero says, use softens even these words which at first seemed harsh.

vi.1-3. Language is based on reason, antiquity, authority, and usage.

There are special rules which must be observed both by speakers and writers. Language is based on reason, antiquity, authority and usage. Reason finds its chief support in analogy and sometimes in etymology. As for antiquity, it is commended to us by the possession of a certain majesty, I might also say sanctity. Authority as a rule we derive from orators and historians. For poets, owing to the necessities of metre, are allowed a certain license. The judgment of a supreme orator is placed on the same level as reason, and even error brings no disgrace, if it result from treading in the footsteps of such distinguished guides. Usage however

---

41. A napkin thrown down by the president of the games as a signal for the races to begin.

42. Strictly speaking Latin was not derived from Greek but was cognate with Greek; i.e., they were sister languages both going back to a common Indo-European ancestor. But Quintilian was certainly correct in indicating the indebtedness of Latin to Greek— as for instance our own English, sprung from Anglo-Saxon as its ancestor, is incalculably indebted to French, Latin, Greek, and other languages and is itself cognate with Latin and Greek.

(Elementary and Secondary Education)   Bk. I.v, vi

is the surest pilot in speaking,[43] and we should treat language as currency minted with the public stamp. But in all these cases we have need of a critical judgment.

vi.28-31 (excerpts). Etymology: definition.

Etymology[44] inquires into the origin of words, and a literal rendering of Greek *etymologia* would be *veriloquium*, a form which even Cicero, its inventor, shrinks from using. Some again, with an eye to the meaning of the word, call it *origination*. Etymology is sometimes of the utmost use, whenever the word under discussion needs interpretation. Consequently we find room for etymology when we are concerned with definitions.[45] Such a science demands profound erudition, whether we are dealing with the large number of words which are derived from the Greek, or are using ancient historians as a basis for inquiry into the origin of names of men, places, nations and cities.

43. We must admire Quintilian's practical acceptance of the guidance of usage as the surest pilot (director) in matters of language. At the same time his statement in the next sentence about the need for critical judgment would indicate that we are not bound to accept everything in linguistic usage as equally good but should seek to ascertain critically what is acceptable and standard (good usage) and what is undesirable or substandard (bad usage)—a task which is still with us today and one which should be pursued relentlessly. See also I.vi.43-45 below.

44. The etymology of "etymology" is Greek *etymos* ("true, real") plus *logos* ("word, discourse, meaning"). Therefore, etymology means the derivation, the true, real, literal, original meaning of a word. So Cicero's *veriloquium: verus* ("true") plus *loquium (loquor,* "speak; a saying").

45. "Whenever a word needs interpretation or definition." What Quintilian says about the value of etymology is, if anything, even more valid for us today where our great English language has such a rich vocabulary derived from many sources. So often in a discussion we have to stop and define our terms (as Socrates would have us do!), and here etymology plays a most fascinating and enlightening role as it does also in the matter of interpretation and nuances. The moral is always to study the etymologies given in dictionaries for a more accurate and vivid understanding. In fact, a course in etymology should be required of *all* education students no matter what grades or subjects they teach because some knowledge of etymology will make any teacher more accurate and more interesting—and will incidentally provide an interesting hobby for life. One despairs of even attempting to illustrate this truth within the limits of an already overgrown footnote, but a little practice in etymology will demonstrate the point. (See any good up-to-date dictionary; Eric Partridge, *Origins, A Short Etymological Dictionary of Modern English,* Macmillan, N.Y., 1959; E. E. Burriss and L. Casson, *Latin and Greek in Current Use,* Prentice-Hall, N.Y., 2nd ed. or later, 1950). However, in a passage omitted because of its difficulties, Quintilian does warn against false etymologies, which we call folk etymologies. Therefore, one should have good authority for any etymologies which he cites.

vi.39-42. Archaic words; authority.

Archaic words not only enjoy the patronage of distinguished authors, but also give style a certain majesty and charm. For they have the authority of age behind them, and for the very reason that they have fallen into desuetude, produce an attractive effect not unlike that of novelty. But such words must be used sparingly and must not thrust themselves upon our notice, since there is nothing more tiresome than affectation, nor above all must they be drawn from remote and forgotten ages. Religion, it is true, forbids us to alter the words of [ancient] hymns and we must treat them as sacred things. But what a faulty thing is speech, whose prime virtue is clearness, if it requires an interpreter to make its meaning plain! Consequently in the case of old words the best will be those that are newest, just as in the case of new words the best will be the oldest.

The same arguments apply to authority. For although the use of words transmitted to us by the best authors may seem to preclude the possibility of error, it is important to notice not merely what they said, but what words they succeeded in sanctioning. For no one to-day would introduce words such as *tuburchinabundus,* "voracious," or *lurchinabundus,* "guzzling," although they have the authority of Cato; nor make *lodices,* "blankets," masculine, though Pollio preferred that gender; nor say *gladiola,* "small swords," though Messala used this plural, nor *parricidatus* for parricide, a form which can scarcely be tolerated even in Caelius, nor will Calvus persuade me to speak of *collos,* "necks." Indeed, were these authors alive to-day, they would never use such words.[46]

vi.43-45. Usage: discussion of what linguistic usage is most appropriate and desirable, a topic still much alive today.

Usage remains to be discussed. For it would be almost laughable to prefer the language of the past to that of the present day, and what is ancient speech but ancient usage of speaking? But even here the critical faculty is necessary, and we must make up our minds what we mean by usage. If it be defined merely as the practice of the majority, we shall have a very dangerous rule

46. Cato lived in the third and second centuries B.C.; the other authors lived in the first century B.C. *Lodices* was regularly feminine; *gladiola* (neut. plu.): the regular form was *gladioli* (masc. plu.); *parricidatus:* the regular form was *parricida, ae, c.; collos:* the regular form was *colla* (neut. plu.).

(Elementary and Secondary Education) Bk. I.vi, vii

affecting not merely style but life as well, a far more serious matter. But where is so much good to be found that what is right should please the majority? The practices of depilation, of dressing the hair in tiers, or of drinking to excess at the baths, although they may have thrust their way into society, cannot claim the support of usage, since there is something to blame in all of them (although we have usage on our side when we bathe or have our hair cut or take our meals together). So too in speech we must not accept as a rule of language words and phrases that have become a vicious habit[47] with a number of persons. To say nothing of the language of the uneducated, we are all of us well aware that whole theatres and the entire crowd of spectators will often commit *barbarisms* in the cries which they utter as one man. I will therefore define usage in speech as the agreed practice of educated men, just as where our way of life is concerned, I should define it as the agreed practice of all good men.

vii.1-4,11. Orthography: the science of writing correctly; i.e., spelling.

Having stated the rules which we must follow in speaking, I will now proceed to lay down the rules which must be observed when we write. Such rules are called *orthography*[48] by the Greeks; let us style it the science of writing correctly. This science does not consist merely in the knowledge of the letters composing each syllable (such a study is beneath the dignity of a teacher of grammar), but, in my opinion, develops all its subtlety in connexion with doubtful points. For instance, while it is absurd to place a circumflex[49] over all long syllables since the quantity of most syllables is obvious from the very nature of the word which is written, it is all the same occasionally necessary, since the same letter involves a different meaning according as it is long or short. For example we determine whether *malus* is to mean an "apple

47. Who can fail to be aware of the bastardization of English in many circles today, as was the case with Latin then. In ancient Rome they called it the language of the *vulgus* (the common people) or vulgar Latin. So today we have our own vulgar and substandard English, which can be more or less understood, to be sure; but it lacks the elegance and beauty and accuracy of the well-disciplined expression which should be expected of all educated people. Vulgar and unacceptable speech is no sign of intelligence or importance. Cp. the last sentence of §45.

48. Orthography: Greek *ortho* ("straight, correct")-*graphia* ("writing"), spelling according to accepted usage.

49. The practice in Latin texts nowadays is to use a long mark, called a macron, over long vowels. See next note.

tree" or a "bad man" by the use of the circumflex;[50] *palus* means a "stake," if the first syllable is long, a "marsh," if it be short; again when the same letter is short in the nominative and long in the ablative, we generally require the circumflex to make it clear which quantity to understand.[51] Similarly it has been held that we should observe distinctions such as the following: if the preposition *ex* is compounded with *specto,* there will be an *s* in the second syllable, while there will be no *s* if it is compounded with *pecto.*[52] Orthography, however, is also the servant of usage and therefore undergoes frequent change.

vii.30-35. Spelling should be essentially phonetic. Although such details are important, let us not be pedantic.

On all such subjects the teacher must use his own judgment; for in such matters it should be the supreme authority. For my own part, I think that, within the limits prescribed by usage, words should be spelt as they are pronounced. For the use of letters is to preserve the sound of words and to deliver them to readers as a sacred trust: consequently they ought to represent the pronunciation which we are to use. These are the more important points in connexion with writing and speaking correctly. I do not go so far as to deny to the teacher of literature all part in the two remaining departments of speaking and writing with elegance and significance, but I reserve these for a more important portion of this work, as I have still to deal with the duties of the teacher of rhetoric.

I am however haunted by the thought that some readers will regard what I have said as trivial details which are only likely to prove a hindrance to those who are intent upon a greater task; and I myself do not think that we should go so far as to lose our sleep of nights or quibble like fools over such minutiae; for such studies make mincemeat of the mind. But it is only the superfluities of grammar that do any harm. I ask you, is Cicero a less great orator for having given this science his diligent attention or for having, as his letters show, demanded rigid correctness of speech from his son? Or was the vigour of Gaius Caesar's elo-

---

50. *Mālus* = "apple tree"; *malus* = "bad man"; *pālus* = "stake"; *palus* = "marsh."

51. E.g., *pecunia* (nominative, or subject, case), "money"; *pecuniā* (ablative), "with or by money."

52. *Ex-specto* = "await"; *ex-pecto* = "comb out."

quence impaired by the publication of a treatise on Analogy? Or the polish of Messala dimmed by the fact that he devoted whole books to the discussion not merely of single words, but of single letters? Such studies do no harm to those who but pass through them: it is only the pedantic stickler who suffers.

viii.1-4. Reading—in our sense of "elocution" with proper understanding and expression. Let students learn not merely what is eloquent but, even more, what is morally excellent.

Reading remains for consideration. In this connexion there is much that can only be taught in actual practice, as for instance when the boy should take breath, at what point he should introduce a pause into a line, where the sense ends or begins, when the voice should be raised or lowered, what modulation should be given to each phrase, and when he should increase or slacken speed, or speak with greater or less energy. In this portion of my work I will give but one golden rule: to do all these things, he must understand what he reads. But above all his reading must be manly, combining dignity and charm; it must be different from the reading of prose, for poetry is song and poets claim to be singers.[53] But this fact does not justify degeneration into sing-song or the effeminate modulations now in vogue: there is an excellent saying on this point attributed to Gaius Caesar while he was still a boy: "If you are singing, you sing badly: if you are reading, you sing." Again I do not, like some teachers, wish character as revealed by speeches to be indicated as it is by the comic actor, though I think that there should be some modulation of the voice to distinguish such passages from those where the poet is speaking in person. There are other points where there is much need of instruction: above all, unformed minds which are liable to be all the more deeply impressed by what they learn in their days of childish ignorance, must learn not merely what is eloquent; it is even more important that they should study what is morally excellent.

---

53. For example, Homer's *Iliad* begins: "Sing to me, O Goddess [=Muse], of the wrath of Achilles"; and Virgil's *Aeneid* begins: "I sing of deeds of arms and a hero." Greek lyric poetry was *sung* to the accompaniment of a lyre; and Horace's lyric poems were called carmina, *songs*)we know them as *odes*, which is a Greek word for song), even though in Roman times they were written to be read or recited rather than sung.

of the grammaticus: epic, tragedy, lyric poetry, comedy; licentious passages to be avoided.

It is therefore an admirable practice which now prevails, to begin by reading Homer and Vergil, although the intelligence needs to be further developed for the full appreciation of their merits: but there is plenty of time for that since the boy will read them more than once. In the meantime let his mind be lifted by the sublimity of heroic verse, inspired by the greatness of its theme and imbued with the loftiest sentiments. The reading of tragedy also is useful, and lyric poets will provide nourishment for the mind, provided not merely the authors be carefully selected, but also the passages from their works which are to be read.[54] For the Greek lyric poets are often licentious and even in Horace there are passages which I should be unwilling to explain to a class. Elegiacs, however, more especially erotic elegy, and hendecasyllables, which are merely sections of Sotadean verse (concerning which latter I need give no admonitions), should be entirely banished, if possible; if not absolutely banished, they should be reserved for pupils of a less impressionable age. As to comedy, whose contribution to eloquence may be of no small importance, since it is concerned with every kind of character and emotion, I will shortly point out in its due place what use can in my opinion be made of it in the education of boys. As soon as we have no fear of contaminating their morals, it should take its place among the subjects which it is specially desirable to read. I speak of Menander, though I would not exclude others. For Latin authors will also be of some service. But the subjects selected for lectures to boys should be those which will enlarge the mind and provide the greatest nourishment to the intellect.[55] Life is quite long enough for the subsequent study of those other subjects which are concerned with matters of interest solely to learned

---

54. Here throughout §6 Quintilian expresses himself emphatically on the problem of the censorship of literature for younger, immature students. Once again, "nothing new under the sun." Today we hear of parents who join Quintilian in censuring textbooks of questionable morality which are assigned to young students by innovating teachers who may, one sometimes feels, enjoy the notoriety of being "far out" and daringly liberal—liberal beyond what the time and the circumstances require, beyond the limits of the appropriate. Sotadean verse just below: Sotades (third century B.C.), Greek writer of indecent satires.

55. Literature to enlarge the mind and nourish the intellect is Quintilian's alternative to morally questionable passages indicated in §6 and note 54 above.

(Elementary and Secondary Education) Bk. I.viii

men. But even the old Latin poets may be of great value, in spite of the fact that their strength lies in their natural talent rather than in their art: above all they will contribute richness of vocabulary: for the vocabulary of the tragedians is full of dignity, while in that of the comedians there is a certain elegance and Attic grace. They are, too, more careful about dramatic structure than the majority of moderns, who regard epigram as the sole merit of every kind of literary work. For purity at any rate and manliness, if I may say so, we must certainly go to these writers, since today even our style of speaking is infected with all the faults of decadence. Finally we may derive confidence from the practice of the greatest orators of drawing upon the early poets to support their arguments or adorn their eloquence. For we find, more especially in the pages of Cicero, but frequently in Asinius and other orators of that period, quotations from Ennius, Accius, Pacuvius, Lucilius, Terence, Caecilius and others, inserted not merely to show the speaker's learning, but to please his hearers as well, since the charms of poetry provide a pleasant relief from the severity of forensic eloquence. Such quotations have the additional advantage of helping the speaker's case, for the orator makes use of the sentiments expressed by the poet as evidence in support of his own statements. But while my earlier remarks have special application to the education of boys, those which I have just made apply rather to persons of riper years; for the love of letters and the value of reading are not confined to one's schooldays, but end only with life.[56]

viii.13-15,17-21. Lectures by the grammaticus on poetry, analyzing the verse, parts of speech, barbarisms, poetic licence, and the positive virtues of the composition and giving an expository account of the various stories that occur. However, the lecturer should avoid superfluous pedantic details.

In lecturing[57] the teacher of literature must give attention to

---

56. Similarly today we find general agreement that education, unending self-education, should continue throughout life starting from "commencement," which marks the beginning of that process.

57. It is interesting to note the antiquity of the lecture method. Be it also noted that the students take at least some part in the session. The efficiency of this combined activity in a smallish class has much to recommend it, and it is used effectively even today despite the sometimes not unjustified hue and cry against lecture courses.

minor points as well; he will ask his class after analysing a verse to give him the parts of speech and the peculiar features of the feet which it contains: these latter should be so familiar in poetry as to make their presence desired even in the prose of oratory. He will point out what words are barbarous, what improperly used, and what are contrary to the laws of language. He will not do this by way of censuring the poets for such peculiarities, for poets are usually the servants of their metres and are allowed such licence that faults are given other names when they occur in poetry. Their aim will rather be to familiarise the pupil with the artifices of style and to stimulate his memory. Further in the elementary stages of such instruction it will not be unprofitable to show the different meanings which may be given to each word. Above all he will impress upon their minds the value of proper arrangement, and of graceful treatment of the matter in hand: he will show what is appropriate to the various characters, what is praiseworthy in the thoughts or words, where copious diction is to be commended and where restraint.

In addition to this he will explain the various stories that occur: this must be done with care, but should not be encumbered with superfluous detail. For it is sufficient to set forth the version which is generally received or at any rate rests upon good authority. But to ferret out everything that has ever been said on the subject even by the most worthless of writers is a sign of tiresome pedantry or empty ostentation,[58] and results in delaying and swamping the mind when it would be better employed on other themes. The man who pores over every page even though it be wholly unworthy of reading, is capable of devoting his attention to the investigation of old wives' tales. And yet the commentaries of teachers of literature are full of such encumbrances to learning and strangely unfamiliar to their own authors. It is, for instance, recorded that Didymus, who was unsurpassed for the number of books which he wrote, on one occasion objected to some story as being absurd, whereupon one of his own books was produced

---

58. We can bless the humanity of Quintilian for inveighing against excessive, tiresome, over zealously detailed scholarship, empty ostentation, and dreary encumbrances to learning in the commentaries of the grammatici. The endless, benumbing loquacity and pedantry of some teachers and scholars in our own times have hurt their causes perhaps more than anything else. The golden mean! And Quintilian's sense of humor in the story about Didymus.

(Elementary and Secondary Education)

which contained the story in question. Such abuses occur chiefly in connexion with fabulous stories and are sometimes carried to ludicrous or even scandalous extremes: for in such cases the more unscrupulous commentator has such full scope for invention, that he can tell lies to his heart's content about whole books and authors without fear of detection: for what never existed can obviously never be found, whereas if the subject is familiar the careful investigator will often detect the fraud. Consequently I shall count it a merit in a teacher of literature that there should be some things which he does not know.

ix.1-6. Composition as taught by the grammaticus for pupils not yet ready for the rhetor (teacher of retoric); the exacting exercise of paraphrasing Aesop's fables; also writing aphorisms, moral essays, and delineations of character.

I have now finished with two of the departments, with which teachers of literature profess to deal, namely the art of speaking correctly and the interpretation of authors; the former they call *methodicē*, the latter *historicē*. We must however add to their activities instruction in certain rudiments of oratory for the benefit of those who are not yet ripe for the schools of rhetoric. Their pupils should learn to paraphrase Aesop's fables, the natural successors of the fairy stories of the nursery, in simple and restrained language and subsequently to set down this paraphrase in writing with the same simplicity of style: they should begin by analysing each verse, then give its meaning in different language, and finally proceed to a freer paraphrase in which they will be permitted now to abridge and now to embellish the original, so far as this may be done without losing the poet's meaning.[59] This is no easy task even for the expert instructor, and the pupil who handles it successfully will be capable of learning everything. He should also be set to write *aphorisms, moral essays (chriae)* and *delineations of character (ethologiae)*, of which the teacher will first give the general scheme, since such themes will be drawn from their reading. In all of these exercises the general idea is the same, but the form differs: *aphorisms* are general propositions, while

---

59. In this exercise of paraphrasing one is somewhat reminded of the valuable and exacting discipline of translating from Latin, or any other language, into English and of trying in the process to say no more and no less than the original says but precisely what the original says. This is a chastening and most instructive experience in the use of one's own mother tongue.

ethologiae are concerned with persons. Of *moral essays* there are various forms: some are akin to *aphorisms* and commence with a simple statement "he said" or "he used to say": others give the answer to a question and begin "on being asked" or "in answer to this he replied," while a third and not dissimilar type begins, "when someone has said or done something." Some hold that a *moral essay* may take some action as its text; take for example the statement "Crates on seeing an ill-educated boy, beat his *paedagogus*," or a very similar example which they do not venture actually to propose as a theme for a *moral essay*, but content themselves with saying that it is of the nature of such a theme, namely "Milo, having accustomed himself to carrying a calf every day, ended by carrying it when grown to a bull." Short stories from the poets should in my opinion be handled not with a view to style but as a means of increasing knowledge. Other more serious and ambitious tasks have been also imposed on teachers of literature by the fact that Latin rhetoricians will have nothing to do with them: Greek rhetoricians have a better comprehension of the extent and nature of the tasks placed on their shoulders.

x.1. Other subjects which are necessary for a general education before the pupil advances from the school of the grammaticus to the school of the rhetor: music, geometry, astronomy.

I have made my remarks on this stage of education as brief as possible, making no attempt to say everything, (for the theme is infinite), but confining myself to the most necessary points. I will now proceed briefly to discuss the remaining arts in which I think boys ought to be instructed before being handed over to the teacher of rhetoric: for it is by such studies that the course of education described by the Greeks as *egkuklios paideia*[60] or general education will be brought to its full completion.

60. *Egkuklios* (or, in Latin, *encyclios*) *paideia* means "a circular (well-rounded, comprehensive) education." Put both words together in a Neo-Latin compound and you end up with *encyclopedia*, which certainly offers a well-rounded education. The etymology and this passage in Quintilian show how old is the concept of a core of general education. The concept of a basic core of general education to be completed by all students as a common experience, a bond for all educated people, and a humanistic, cultural background for any specialized or vocational studies—that concept appeals to many as still valid and essential today. To be sure, we well know that any required, well-structured core curriculum and any courses which might contain any knowledge of, and acknowledgment of, any indebtedness to the values and experiences of the past—we know that such courses and curricula are currently being denounced with loud voice by certain callow youth

(Elementary and Secondary Education) Bk. I.ix, x

x.2-8. Heated debate over whether such subjects as music, geometry, and astronomy are essential courses in a curriculum leading to oratory.

For their are other subjects of education which must be studied simultaneously with literature. These being independent studies are capable of completion without a knowledge of oratory, while on the other hand they cannot by themselves produce an orator. The question has consequently been raised as to whether they are necessary for this purpose. What, say some, has the knowledge of the way to describe an equilateral triangle on a given straight line got to do with pleading in the law-courts or speaking in the senate? Will an acquaintance with the names and intervals of the notes of the lyre help an orator to defend a criminal or direct the policy of his country? They will perhaps produce a long list of orators who are most effective in the courts but have never sat under a geometrician and whose understanding of music is confined to the pleasure which their ears, like those of other men, derive from it. To such critics I reply, and Cicero frequently makes the same remark in his Orator, that I am not describing any orator who actually exists or has existed, but have in my mind's eye an ideal orator, perfect down to the smallest detail. For when the philosophers describe the ideal sage who is to be consummate in all knowledge and a very god incarnate, as they say, they would have him receive instruction not merely in the knowledge of things human and divine, but would also lead him through a course of subjects, which in themselves are comparatively trivial, as for instance the elaborate subtleties of formal logic: not that acquaintance with the so called "horn"[61] or "crocodile"[62] problems can make a man wise, but because it is important that he should never trip even in the smallest trifles. So

and special interest groups who demand the abolition of academic requirements and the dilution of intellectual disciplines and standards. However, if we can grant that sanity will survive in the academic world and in society, the concept of a general education core will continue, but we shall no doubt for a long time see educational ferment at work from institution to institution and even within institutions concerning what courses are to be included in a core curriculum, and why and how. Let us prepare ourselves for this continuing debate. So here we are back again with Quintilian and his debate with his antagonists in Chapter X.

61. A sophistic argument in the form of syllogism. "You have what you have not lost. You have not lost horns. Therefore you have horns."

62. A sophism which goes as follows. A crocodile, having seized a woman's son, said that he would restore him to her if she would tell him the truth. She replied, "You will not restore him." Was it the crocodile's duty to restore him?

too the teacher of geometry, music or other subjects which I would class with these, will not be able to create the perfect orator (who like the philosopher ought to be a wise man), but none the less these arts will assist in his perfection. I may draw a parallel from the use of antidotes and other remedies applied to the eyes or to wounds. We know that these are composed of ingredients which produce many and sometimes contrary effects, but mixed together they make a single compound resembling no one of its component parts, but deriving its peculiar properties from all: so too dumb insects produce honey, whose taste is beyond the skill of man to imitate, from different kinds of flowers and juices. Shall we marvel then, if oratory, the highest gift of providence to man, needs the assistance of many arts, which, although they do not reveal or intrude themselves in actual speaking, supply hidden forces and make their silent presence felt? "But" it will be urged "men have proved fluent without their aid." Granted, but I am in quest of an orator. "Their contribution is but small." Yes, but we shall never attain completeness, if minor details be lacking. And it will be agreed that though our ideal of perfection may dwell on a height that is hard to gain, it is our duty to teach all we know that achievement may at least come somewhat nearer the goal. But why should our courage fail? The perfect orator is not contrary to the laws of nature, and it is cowardly to despair of anything that is within the bounds of possibility.

x.9-10,14-21. *Music: its importance in education from the earliest times on.*

For myself I should be ready to accept the verdict of antiquity. Who is ignorant of the fact that music, of which I will speak first, was in ancient times the object not merely of intense study but of veneration: in fact Orpheus and Linus, to mention no others, were regarded as uniting the roles of musician, poet and philosopher. Both were of divine origin, while the former, because by the marvel of his music he soothed the savage breast, is recorded to have drawn after him not merely beasts of the wild, but rocks and trees.[63] So too Timagenes[64] asserts that music is the oldest of the arts related to literature, a statement which is confirmed by the testimony of the greatest of poets in whose songs we

63. For the power of music and a reference to Orpheus see Dryden's *A Song for St. Cecilia's Day*; and also his *Alexander's Feast; or The Power of Music*.
64. A Greek rhetorician who was taken to Rome in 55 B.C.

read that the praises of heroes and of gods were sung to the music of the lyre at the feasts of kings. It is recorded that the greatest generals played on the lyre and the pipe, and the armies of Sparta were fired to martial ardour by the strains of music. And what else is the function of the horns and trumpets attached to our legions? The louder the concert of their notes, the greater is the glorious supremacy of our arms over all the nations of the earth. It was not therefore without reason that Plato regarded the knowledge of music as necessary to his ideal statesman or politician, as he calls him; while the leaders even of that school, which in other respects is the strictest and most severe of all schools of philosophy,[65] held that the wise man might well devote some of his attention to such studies. Lycurgus himself, the founder of the stern laws of Sparta, approved of the training supplied by music. Indeed nature itself seems to have given music as a boon to men to lighten the strain of labour: even the rower in the galleys is cheered to effort by song. Nor is this function of music confined to cases where the efforts of a number are given union by the sound of some sweet voice that sets the tune, but even solitary workers find solace at their toil in artless song. So far I have attempted merely to sound the praises of the noblest of arts without bringing it into connexion with the education of an orator. I will therefore pass by the fact that the art of letters and that of music were once united.[66] Aristophanes again in more than one of his plays shows that boys were trained in music from remote antiquity, while in the *Hypobolimaeus* of Menander an old man, when a father claims his son from him, gives an account of all expenses incurred on behalf of the boy's education and states that he has paid out large sums to musicians and geometricians. From the importance thus given to music also originated the custom of taking a lyre round the company after dinner, and when on such an occasion Themistocles confessed that he could not play, his education was (to quote the words of Cicero) "regarded as imperfect." Even at the banquets of our own forefathers it was the custom to introduce the pipe and lyre, and even the hymn of the Salii has its tune. These practices were instituted by King Numa and clearly prove that not even those whom we regard as rude warriors, neglected the study of music, at least in so far as the resources of that age allowed. Finally there

65. Namely, the Stoics.
66. See note 53 above.

was actually a proverb among the Greeks, that the uneducated were far from the company of the Muses and Graces.[67]

x.22-33. Music: its specific values and powers.

But let us discuss the advantages which our future orator may reasonably expect to derive from the study of Music. Music has two modes of expression in the voice and in the body;[68] for both voice and body require to be controlled by appropriate rules. Aristoxenus divides music, in so far as it concerns the voice, into *rhythm* and *melody*, the one consisting in measure, the latter in sound and song. Now I ask you whether it is not absolutely necessary for the orator to be acquainted with all these methods of expression which are concerned firstly with gesture, secondly with the arrangement of words and thirdly with the inflexions of the voice, of which a great variety are required in pleading. Otherwise we must assume that structure and the euphonious combination of sounds are necessary only for poetry, lyric and otherwise, but superfluous in pleading, or that unlike music, oratory has no interest in the variation of arrangement and sound to suit the demands of the case. But eloquence does vary both tone and rhythm, expressing sublime thoughts with elevation, pleasing thoughts with sweetness, and ordinary with gentle utterance, and in every expression of its art is in sympathy with the emotions of which it is the mouth-piece. It is by the raising, lowering or inflexion of the voice that the orator stirs the emotions of his hearers, and the measure, if I may repeat the term, of voice or phrase differs according as we wish to rouse the indignation or the pity of the judge. For, as we know, different emotions are roused even by the various musical instruments, which are incapable of reproducing speech. Further the motion of the body must be suitable and becoming, or as the Greeks call it *eurythmic*, and this can only be secured by the study of music. This is a most important department of eloquence, and will receive separate treatment in this work. To proceed, an orator will assuredly pay special attention to his voice, and what is so specially the concern of music as this? Here too I must not anticipate a later section of

---

67. The Muses, ultimately nine in number, were goddesses who presided over artistic and intellectual activities such as literature, music, dance, astronomy. The Graces, usually three in number, were goddesses personifying beauty, charm, and grace be it physical, intellectual, artistic, moral.

68. I.e., dancing or at least graceful movements.

this work, and will content myself by citing the example of Gaius Gracchus, the leading orator of his age, who during his speeches had a musician standing behind him with a pitchpipe, or *tonarion* as the Greeks call it, whose duty it was to give him the tones in which his voice was to be pitched. Such was the attention which he paid to this point even in the midst of his most turbulent speeches, when he was terrifying the patrician party and even when he had begun to fear their power. I should like for the benefit of the uninstructed, those "creatures of the heavier Muse," as the saying is, to remove all doubts as to the value of music. They will at any rate admit that the poets should be read by our future orator. But can they be read without some knowledge of music? Or if any of my critics be so blind as to have some doubts about other forms of poetry, can the lyric poets at any rate be read without such knowledge? If there were anything novel in my insistence on the study of music, I should have to treat the matter at great length. But in view of the fact that the study of music has, from those remote times when Chiron taught Achilles down to our own day, continued to be studied by all except those who have a hatred for any regular course of study,[69] it would be a mistake to seem to cast any doubt upon its value by showing an excessive zeal in its defence. It will, however, I think be sufficiently clear from the examples I have already quoted, what I regard as the value and the sphere of music in the training of an orator. Still I think I ought to be more emphatic than I have been in stating that the music which I desire to see taught is not our modern music, which has been emasculated by the lascivious melodies of our effeminate stage and has to no small extent destroyed such manly vigour as we still possessed. No, I refer to the music of old which was employed to sing the praises of brave men and was sung by the brave themselves. I will have none of your psalteries and viols, that are unfit even for the use of a modest girl. Give me the knowledge of the principles of music, which have power to excite or assuage the emotions of mankind.[70] We are told that Pythagoras on one occasion, when some young men were led

---

69. So there have always been, and not merely in our own times, some people who are averse to reasonable and adequate discipline, to "a regular course of study." They fail to realize that no worthwhile human achievement can be accomplished without great labor and without well-directed effort, which is called discipline, i.e., training and learning.

70. Again see Dryden's *Alexander's Feast; or The Power of Music.*

astray by their passions to commit an outrage on a respectable family, calmed them by ordering the piper to change her strain to a spondaic measure, while Chrysippus selects a special tune to be used by nurses to entice their little charges to sleep. Further I may point out that among the fictitious themes employed in declamation is one, doing no little credit to its author's learning, in which it is supposed that a piper is accused of manslaughter because he had played a tune in the Phrygian mode as an accompaniment to a sacrifice, with the result that the person officiating went mad and flung himself over a precipice. If an orator is expected to declaim on such a theme as this, which cannot possibly be handled without some knowledge of music, how can my critics for all their prejudice fail to agree that music is a necessary element in the education of an orator?

x.34-37. Geometry comprises numbers (our mathematics) and geometric forms (our geometry). It exercises the mind and sharpens perception. Mathematics is absolutely essential for all, even in an elementary education, and linear geometry can be helpful. Geometry teaches the necessity of logical development by arguing from definite premises to conclusions which had been previously uncertain.

As regards geometry,[71] it is granted that portions of this science are of value for the instruction of children: for admittedly it exercises their minds, sharpens their wits and generates quickness of perception.[72] But it is considered that the value of geometry resides in the process of learning, and not as with

---

71. By "geometry" Quintilian here clearly means all mathematics as is shown by his "two divisions" of gemoetry in §35 below.

72. Quintilian's belief in the educational value of mathematics and geometry ("It exercises their minds, sharpens their wits and generates quickness of perception") has continued down to our own times, as has "the general opinion" that the value of geometry resides in the process of learning and not the knowledge acquired (though the practical Roman was frankly more likely to be interested in utility than in mere theory). All this is roughly what we currently call "the old math," which has proved beneficial to students for a long time. "The new math" was introduced into some schools in the 1950's amid our current educational ferment and passion for novelty; and as in the case of so many new schemes, its promoters sought to throw out the old math, good practices and all. Many feel that the new math will have to be considerably revamped before it can be made really valuable and meaningful to young students and can demonstrate that it can accomplish more and better than the old math. One hopes that the new math will not hurt a generation of students as did the "whole-word" method of learning to read, which proved so disastrous. (See Donald Barr, *Who Pushed Humpty Dumpty*, "Mathematics Is. . ." pp. 269-278. See also *Why Johnny Can't Add* by Morris Kline.)

(Elementary and Secondary Education) Bk. I.x

other sciences in the knowledge thus acquired. Such is the general opinion. But it is not without good reason that some of the greatest men have devoted special attention to this science. Geometry has two divisions; one is concerned with numbers, the other with figures.[73] Now knowledge of the former is a necessity not merely to the orator, but to any one who has had even an elementary education. Such knowledge is frequently required in actual cases, in which a speaker is regarded as deficient in education, I will not say if he hesitates in making a calculation, but even if he contradicts the calculation which he states in words by making an uncertain or inappropriate gesture with his fingers.[74] Again linear geometry is frequently required in cases, as in lawsuits about boundaries and measurements. But geometry and oratory are related in a yet more important way than this. In the first place logical development is one of the necessities of geometry. And is it not equally a necessity for oratory? Geometry arrives at its conclusions from definite premises, and by arguing from what is certain proves what was previously uncertain. Is not this just what we do in speaking?

x.46-48. Astronomy, geometry in the heavens.

But geometry soars still higher to the consideration of the system of the universe: for by its calculations it demonstrates the fixed and ordained courses of the stars, and thereby we acquire the knowledge that all things are ruled by order and destiny, a consideration which may at times be of value to an orator. When Pericles dispelled the panic caused at Athens by the eclipse of the sun by explaining the causes of the phenomenon, or Sulpicius Gallus discoursed on the eclipse of the moon to the army of Lucius Paulus to prevent the soldiers being seized with terror at what they regarded as a portent sent by heaven, did not they discharge the function of an orator? If Nicias had known this when he commanded in Sicily, he would not have shared the terror of his men nor lost the finest army that Athens ever placed in the field. Dion for instance when he came to Syracuse to overthrow the tyranny of Dionysius, was not frightened away by the occurrence of a similar phenomenon.

xi.1-3. The actor can help the orator in the matter of delivery, but there are some things which the young pupil should not imitate.

73. I.e., geometric shapes.
74. Roman numerals were so clumsy to use in arithmetic that the Romans learned to count on their fingers in an elaborate way, and also to use an abacus.

The comic actor will also claim a certain amount of our attention, but only in so far as our future orator must be a master of the art of delivery.[75] For I do not of course wish the boy, whom we are training to this end, to talk with the shrillness of a woman or in the tremulous accents of old age. Nor for that matter must he ape the vices of the drunkard, or copy the cringing manners of a slave, or learn to express the emotions of love, avarice or fear. Such accomplishments are not necessary to an orator and corrupt the mind, especially while it is still pliable and unformed. For repeated imitation passes into habit. Nor yet again must we adopt all the gestures and movements of the actor. Within certain limits the orator must be a master of both, but he must rigorously avoid staginess and all extravagance of facial expression, gesture and gait. For if an orator does command a certain art in such matters, its highest expression will be in the concealment of its existence.

xi.4,8-14. The first duty of the actor teacher is to correct faults of pronunciation and teach proper traits of speech, gestures, and facial expression. To teach various types of delivery the actor should require the student to learn select passages by heart and declaim them properly. Thus he will simultaneously train delivery, voice, and memory.

What then is the duty of the teacher whom we have borrowed from the stage? In the first place he must correct all faults of pronunciation, and see that the utterance is distinct, and that each letter has its proper sound.[76] He will also see that final syllables are not clipped,[77] that the quality of speech is continuously main-

---

75. Cp. Cicero, *de Oratore*, I.lix: Antonius says, "Who can deny that the gesture and grace of Roscius [a very famous actor at Rome] are necessary in the orator's action and deportment?"

76. Sad to say, some teachers no less than students are careless about pronouncing accurately, clearly, and distinctly. Everybody should be more careful about this. Consider, for example, the delight of listening to the careful, clear, well-modulated, well-disciplined action of our finest actors and broadcasters.

77. Incidentally, this trend of neglecting or dropping the final inflected endings of words continued in the vulgar (*vulgus* = the common people) Latin of the common people to the point, about A.D. 800, where Latin was no longer Latin but became a Romance language such as French, Italian, Spanish, Portuguese. However, be it noted that Latin proper, with some ups and downs, remained the language of the cultural, the intellectual, the religious, the scientific, the legal, and the political worlds for centuries and thus served as a uniting lingua franca throughout the occidental world. In fact, it so remained down to the time when Dante early in the fourteenth century decided to compose his *Divine Comedy* in the Italian vernacular rather than in the erstwhile literary language, Latin. Even after that Latin survived throughout the Renaissance and somewhat thereafter as a

(Elementary and Secondary Education) Bk. I.xi 73

tained, that when the voice is raised, the strain falls upon the lungs and not the mouth, and that gesture and voice are mutually appropriate. He will also insist that the speaker faces his audience, that the lips are not distorted nor the jaws parted to a grin, that the face is not thrown back, nor the eyes fixed on the ground, nor the neck slanted to left or right. For there are a variety of faults of facial expression. I have seen many who raised their brows whenever the voice was called upon for an effort, others who wore a perpetual frown, and yet others who could not keep their eyebrows level, but raised one towards the top of the head and depressed the other till it almost closed the eye. These are details, but as I shall shortly show, they are of enormous importance, for nothing that is unbecoming can have a pleasing effect.

Our actor will also be required to show how a narrative should be delivered, and to indicate the authoritative tone that should be given to advice, the excitement which should mark the rise of anger, and the change of tone that is characteristic of pathos. The best method of so doing is to select special passages from comedy appropriate for the purpose, that is to say, resembling the speeches of a pleader. These are not only most useful in training the delivery, but are admirably adapted to increase a speaker's eloquence. These are the methods to be employed while the pupil is too young to take in more advanced instruction; but when the time has come for him to read speeches, and as soon as he begins to appreciate their merits, he should have a careful and efficient teacher at his side not merely to form his style of reading aloud, but to make him learn select passages by heart and declaim them standing in the manner which actual pleading would require: thus he will simultaneously train delivery, voice and memory.

xi.15-19. The teacher of gymnastics can help in the proper movement of arms, hands, feet, head, eyes.

I will not blame even those who give a certain amount of time to the teacher of gymnastics. I am not speaking of those who spend part of their life in rubbing themselves with oil and part in

viable language in many circles. Question: Was Quintilian wrong in insisting on linguistic discipline and excellence for at least the educated in his times, and need we apologize for insisting on a system of education which provides discipline and excellence in the accurate and effective use of our own language, our most important tool in the vital battle of communications and thus of human understanding?

wine-bibbing, and kill the mind by over-attention to the body: indeed, I would have such as these kept as far as possible from the boy whom we are training. But we give the same name to those who form gesture and motion so that the arms may be extended in the proper manner, the management of the hands free from all trace of rusticity and inelegance, the attitude becoming, the movements of the feet appropriate and the motions of the head and eyes in keeping with the poise of the body. No one will deny that such details form a part of the art of delivery, nor divorce delivery from oratory; and there can be no justification for disdaining to learn what has got to be done, especially as *chironomy,* which, as the name shows, is *the law of gesture,* originated in heroic times and met with the approval of the greatest Greeks, not excepting Socrates himself, while it was placed by Plato among the virtues of a citizen and included by Chrysippus in his instructions relative to the education of children. We are told that the Spartans even regarded a certain form of dance as a useful element in military training. Nor again did the ancient Romans consider such a practice as disgraceful: this is clear from the fact that priestly and ritual dances have survived to the present day, while Cicero in the third book of his *de Oratore*[78] quotes the words of Crassus, in which he lays down the principle that the orator "should learn to move his body in a bold and manly fashion derived not from actors or the stage, but from martial and even from gymnastic exercises." And such a method of training has persisted uncensured to our own time. In my opinion, however, such training should not extend beyond the years of boyhood, and even boys should not devote too much time to it. For I do not wish the gestures of oratory to be modelled on those of the dance. But I do desire that such boyish exercises should continue to exert a certain influence, and that something of the grace which we acquired as learners should attend us in after life without our being conscious of the fact.

xii.1-7. Question: Can all the above-mentioned subjects of Quintilian's curriculum be taken simultaneously? Critics claim that is not right to put such a burden on boys of the secondary school age. Quintilian effectively refutes these critics by showing that the human mind requires variety and is dulled by monotony.

The question is not infrequently asked, as to whether, admit-

---

78. *De Oratore,* III.lix.

(Elementary and Secondary Education)   Bk. I.xi, xii

ting that these things ought to be learned, it is possible for all of them to be taught and taken in simultaneously. There are some who say that this is impossible on the ground that the mind is confused and tired by application to so many studies of different tendencies: neither the intelligence nor the physique of our pupils, nor the time at our disposal are sufficient, they say, and even though older boys may be strong enough, it is a sin to put such a burden on the shoulders of childhood. These critics show 2 an insufficient appreciation of the capacities of the human mind, which is so swift and nimble and versatile, that it cannot be restricted to doing one thing only, but insists on devoting its attention to several different subjects not merely in one day, but actually at one and the same time. Do not harpists simultaneously 3 exert the memory and pay attention to the tone and inflexions of the voice, while the right hand runs over certain strings and the left plucks, stops or releases others, and even the foot is employed in beating time, all these actions being performed at the same moment? Again, do not we ourselves, when unexpectedly called 4 upon to plead, speak while we are thinking what we are to say next, invention of argument, choice of words, rhythm, gesture, delivery, facial expression and movement all being required simultaneously? If all these things can be done with one effort in spite of their diversity, why should we not divide our hours among different branches of study? We must remember that variety serves to refresh and restore the mind, and that it is really considerably harder to work at one subject without intermission. Consequently we should give the pen a rest by turning to read, and relieve the tedium of reading by changes of subject. However 5 manifold our activities, in a certain sense we come fresh to each new subject. Who can maintain his attention, if he has to listen for a whole day to one teacher harping on the same subject, be it what it may? Change of studies is like change of foods: the stomach is refreshed by their variety and derives greater nourishment from variety of viands. If my critics disagree, let 6 them provide me with an alternative method. Are we first to deliver ourselves up to the sole service of the teacher of literature, and then similarly to the teacher of geometry, neglecting under the latter what was taught us by the former? And then are we to go on to the musician, forgetting all that we learned before? And when we study Latin literature, are we to do so to the exclusion of

Greek? In fine, to have done with the matter once and for all, are we to do nothing except that which last comes to our hand? On this principle, why not advise farmers not to cultivate corn, vines, olives and orchard trees at the same time? or from devoting themselves simultaneously to pastures, cattle, gardens, bees and poultry? Why do we ourselves daily allot some of our time to the business of the courts, some to the demands of our friends, some to our domestic affairs, some to the exercise of the body, and some even to our pleasures? Any one of these occupations, if pursued without interruption, would fatigue us. So much easier is it to do many things than to do one thing for a long time continuously.

xii.8-11. Furthermore, boys will not find their work too exhausting, for (1) there is no age more capable of enduring fatigue; (2) the mind is easier to teach before it is set (e.g., in learning a language); (3) boys stand the strain of work better than young men do because their activity demands less exertion of their own in as much as they are simply required pliably and docilely to follow the path determined by the teacher. The senses are less affected by mere hard work than they are by hard thinking.

We need have no fear at any rate that boys will find their work too exhausting: there is no age more capable of enduring fatigue. The fact may be surprising, but it can be proved by experiment. For the mind is all the easier to teach before it is set. This may be clearly proved by the fact that within two years after a child has begun to form words correctly, he can speak practically all without any pressure from outside. On the other hand how many years it takes for our newly-imported slaves to become familiar with the Latin language. Try to teach an adult to read and you will soon appreciate the force of the saying applied to those who do everything connected with their art with the utmost skill "he started young!" Moreover boys stand the strain of work better than young men. Just as small children suffer less damage from their frequent falls, from their crawling on hands and knees and, a little later, from their incessant play and their running about from morn till eve, because they are so light in weight and have so little to carry, even so their minds are less susceptible of fatigue, because their activity calls for less effort and application to study demands no exertion of their own, since they are merely so much plastic material to be moulded by the teacher. And further owing to the general pliability of childhood, they follow their instructors

(Elementary and Secondary Education) Bk. I.xii

with greater simplicity and without attempting to measure their own progress: for as yet they do not even appreciate the nature of their work. Finally, as I have often noticed, the senses are less affected by mere hard work than they are by hard thinking.

xii.12-14. Finally, this is the best period for such studies since, when the student has progressed to more creative subjects, he will have neither time nor inclination for these foundation subjects, the benefits of which he will need.

Moreover there will never be more time for such studies, since at this age all progress is made through listening to the teacher. Later when the boy has to write by himself, or to produce and compose something out of his own head, he will neither have the time nor the inclination for the exercises which we have been discussing. Since, then, the teacher of literature neither can nor ought to occupy the whole day, for fear of giving his pupil a distaste for work, what are the studies to which the spare time should preferably be devoted? For I do not wish the student to wear himself out in such pursuits: I would not have him sing or learn to read music or dive deep into the minuter details of geometry, nor need he be a finished actor in his delivery or a dancer in his gesture: if I did demand all these accomplishments, there would yet be time for them; the period allotted to education is long, and I am not speaking of duller wits.

xii.16-19. The plea of the difficulty of the subject is intended as a cloak for our laziness and our desire to take shortcuts to quick riches. Quintilian appeals stirringly to the noble, ideal, non-monetary, professional concept or oratory (eloquence) as the regina rerum, pulcherrima rerum.

The plea of the difficulty of the subject is put forward merely to cloak our indolence, because we do not love the work that lies before us nor seek to win eloquence for our own[79] because it is a noble art and the fairest thing in all the world, but gird up our loins for mercenary ends and for the winning of filthy lucre. Without such accomplishments many may speak in the courts and make an income; but it is my prayer that every dealer in the vilest merchandise may be richer than they and that the public crier may find his voice a more lucrative possession.[80] And I trust that

---

79. Or "for its own sake."
80. Businessmen go into business because it is their avowed purpose to make money; and so it seems appropriate for them to have material success. But Quintilian, in keeping with the older Roman *theory* that an orator was not to be *paid*

there is not one even among my readers who would think of calculating the monetary value of such studies. But he that has enough of the divine spark to conceive the ideal eloquence, he who, as the great tragic poet says, regards "oratory" as "the queen of all the world" and seeks not the transitory gains of advocacy, but those stable and lasting rewards which his own soul and knowledge and contemplation can give, *he* will easily persuade himself to spend his time not, like so many, in the theatre or in the Campus Martius, in dicing or in idle talk, to say naught of the hours that are wasted in sleep or long drawn banqueting, but in listening rather to the geometrician and the teacher of music. For by this he will win a richer harvest of delight than can ever be gathered from the pleasures of the ignorant, since among the many gifts of providence to man not the least is this that the highest pleasure is the child of virtue.[81] But the attractions of my theme have led me to say overmuch. Enough of those studies in which a boy must be instructed, while he is yet too young to proceed to greater things! My next book will start afresh and will pass to the consideration of the duties of the teacher of rhetoric.

---

for his services but was to act in the spirit of noblesse oblige, says in effect that the motives of the Roman orator at his best should be more noble and idealistic and should not be concerned with mere monetary profits; for the true orator experiences satisfactions which transcend pecuniary and material success. In this setting one is tempted to contrast on the one hand those who devote themselves to teaching as a calling (vocation) to serve their fellow men with, on the other hand, those whose prime concern in considering the field of teaching is "How much money can I make at this job and what are the fringe benefits?"

81. Literally, "noble activities provide greater pleasure." This whole passage (§§17-18) also emphasizes the desirability of a good liberal education for its own sake.

BOOK II

CHAPTERS I-XIII, XVI, XIX, XXI

(Higher Education)

i.1-6. The grammaticus and the rhetor.[1] *Often boys could enter the school of the rhetor earlier than they do because the grammaticus increasingly encroaches on the field of the rhetor and provides instruction in* prosopopoeiae *(declamations regarding character) and* suasoriae *(declamations on deliberative themes), which really belong to the first stages of rhetoric. The two professions must be assigned their proper spheres: "grammatice" deals with the* theory of correct speech; *"rhetorice," with the* power of eloquence.

1. A summary review of Book I will provide a background for Quintilian's statements here at the beginning of Book II. At the age of six or seven the boy progresses from the nurse and "nursery school" age to the elementary school under the ludi magister, or litterator, where he learns among other things to write and read correctly and with some facility. At the age of twelve or or thirteen the boy enters the school of the grammaticus, which is roughly equivalent to our secondary or high school. The grammaticus teaches both the Greek and the Latin languages (various aspects of linguistic studies) and literatures (primarily the analysis, explication, and appreciation of poetry); and the boy becomes adept at clear, correct speaking and composition and interpretation of the poets. He also studies a certain amount of geometry, astronomy, music, and gesturing, and he memorizes much. Such is the regular curriculum of the secondary school of the grammaticus. Finally, at about the age of sixteen the young man goes on to college, i.e., the school of the rhetor, whose instruction deals with the power and practice of eloquence. But it seems that some students, at any rate, enter the school of the rhetor with a sort of "advanced standing," having been already instructed by the grammaticus in certain types of declamations which are supposed to be the first rhetorical exercise performed under the rhetor.

The custom has prevailed and is daily growing commoner of sending boys to the schools of rhetoric much later than is reasonable: this is always the case as regards Latin rhetoric and occasionally applies to Greek as well. The reason for this is twofold: the rhetoricians, more especially our own, have abandoned certain of their duties and the teachers of literature have undertaken tasks which rightly belong to others. For the rhetorician considers that his duty is merely to declaim and give instruction in the theory and practice of declamation[2] and confines his activities to deliberative and judicial themes, regarding all others as beneath the dignity of his profession; while the teacher of literature is not satisfied to take what is left him (and we owe him a debt of gratitude for this), but even presumes to handle declamations in character and deliberative themes, tasks which impose the very heaviest burden on the speaker. Consequently subjects which once formed the first stages of rhetoric have come to form the final stages of a literary education, and boys who are ripe for more advanced study are kept back in the inferior[3] school and practise rhetoric under the direction of teachers of literature. Thus we get the absurd result that a boy is not regarded as fit to go on to the schools of declamation till he knows how to declaim.

The two professions must each be assigned their proper sphere. *Grammatice*,[4] which we translate as the *science of letters*, must learn to know its own limits, especially as it has encroached so far beyond the boundaries to which its unpretentious name should restrict it and to which its earlier professors actually confined themselves. Springing from a tiny fountain-head, it has gathered strength from the historians and critics and has swollen to the dimensions of a brimming river, since, not content with the theory of correct speech, no inconsiderable subject, it has usurped the study of practically all the highest departments of knowledge. On the other hand rhetoric, which derives its name from the power of *eloquence*, must not shirk its peculiar duties nor rejoice to see its own burdens shouldered by others. For the neglect of these is little less than a surrender of its birthright. I will

2. Declamation: exercise in oratorical (rhetorical) delivery.
3. Since "inferior" here might be read in an unduly pejorative sense, perhaps a better translation of the Latin *minore* would be "lower" or "secondary."
4. *Grammatice* (sc. *techne*, "art, skill, science") is the science of language and literature, especially poetry, taught by the grammaticus.

of course admit that there may be a few professors of literature who have acquired sufficient knowledge to be able to teach rhetoric as well; but when they do so, they are performing the duties of the rhetorician, not their own.

i.7-13. When should a boy be turned over to the rhetor for instruction? When he is fit—not so much by age as by training—to undertake the first rhetorical exercises; e.g., to compose narratives and passages of praise or denunciation. In fact, it is possible for a boy to study under both a grammaticus and a rhetor at the same time.

A further point into which we must enquire concerns the age at which a boy may be considered sufficiently advanced to profit by the instructions of the rhetorician. In this connexion we must consider not the boy's actual age but the progress he has made in his studies. To put it briefly, I hold that the best answer to the question "When should a boy be sent to the school of rhetoric?" is this, "When he is fit." But this question is really dependent on that previously raised. For if the duties of the teacher of literature are prolonged to include instruction in deliberative declamation, this will postpone the need for the rhetorician. On the other hand if the rhetorician does not refuse to undertake the first duties of his task, his instruction will be required from the moment the boy begins to compose narratives and his first attempts at passages of praise or denunciation. We know that the orators of earlier days improved their eloquence by declaiming themes[5] and common-places[6] and other forms of rhetorical exercises not involving particular circumstances or persons such as provide the material for real or imaginary causes. From this we can clearly see what a scandalous dereliction of duty it is for the schools of rhetoric to abandon this department of their work, which was not merely its first, but for a long time its sole task. What is there in those exercises of which I have just spoken that does not involve matters which are the special concern of rhetoric and further are typical of actual legal cases? Have we not to narrate facts in the law-courts? Indeed I am not sure that this is not the most impor-

---

5. Themes: the word in the Latin text here is *theses,* which in other passages Butler usually renders as "theses" (e.g., in II.iv.24 below, where theses are further discussed). Theses are general questions suitable for debate, commonly involving a comparison (e.g., Which is preferable, town or country life?)

6. Common-places are moral questions in which vices are denounced without attacking particular persons. See II.iv.22 below.

tant department of rhetoric in actual practice. Are not eulogy and denunciation frequently introduced in the course of the contests of the courts? Are not *common-places* frequently inserted in the very heart of lawsuits, whether like those which we find in the works of Cicero, they are directed against vice, or, like those published by Quintus Hortensius, deal with questions of general interest such as "whether small points of argument should carry weight," or are employed to defend or impugn the credibility of witnesses? These are weapons which we should always have stored in our armoury ready for immediate use as occasion may demand. The critic who denies that such matters concern an orator is one who will refuse to believe that a statue is being begun when its limbs are actually being cast.[7] Some will think that I am in too great a hurry, but let no one accuse me of thinking that the pupil who has been entrusted to the rhetorician should forthwith be withdrawn from the teacher of literature. The latter will still have certain hours allotted him, and there is no reason to fear that a boy will be overloaded by receiving instruction from two different masters.[8] It will not mean any increase of work, but merely the division among two masters of the studies which were previously indiscriminately combined under one: and the efficiency of either teacher will be increased.[9] This method is still in vogue among the Greeks, but has been abandoned by us, not perhaps without some excuse, as there were others ready to step into the rhetorician's shoes.

ii.1-8. Choice of a teacher of rhetoric: emphasis on the prime importance of his character; and a magnificent portrayal of the ideal teacher, which deserves to be read over and over—and pondered.

As soon therefore as a boy has made sufficient progress in his studies to be able to follow what I have styled the first stage of instruction in rhetoric, he should be placed under a rhetorician. Our first task must be to enquire whether the teacher is of good character.[10] The reason which leads me to deal with this subject in

---

7. Commonly the parts of a bronze statue were cast separately and then soldered together.

8. Cp. I.xii.1ff. above.

9. Cp. I.xii.4-5,13 above.

10. Quintilian's repeated emphasis on the need of good character in a teacher was especially important and necessary amid the corruptions of imperial Rome (e.g., I.i.4 above and note 3 thereon; I.ii.4-8 above; II.ii.14-15 below) Are our times much better?

this portion of my work is not that I regard character as a matter of indifference where other teachers are concerned, (I have already shown how important I think it in the preceding book), but that the age to which the pupil has now attained makes the mention of this point especially necessary. For as a rule boys are on the verge of manhood when transferred to the teacher of rhetoric and continue with him even when they are young men: consequently we must spare no effort to secure that the purity of the teacher's character should preserve those of tenderer years from corruption, while its authority should keep the bolder spirits from breaking out into licence. Nor is it sufficient that he should merely set an example of the highest personal self-control; he must also be able to govern the behaviour of his pupils by the strictness of his discipline.

Let him therefore adopt a parental attitude to his pupils, and regard himself as the representative of those who have committed their children to his charge. Let him be free from vice himself and refuse to tolerate it in others. Let him be strict but not austere, genial but not too familiar: for austerity will make him unpopular, while familiarity breeds contempt. Let his discourse continually turn on what is good and honourable; the more he admonishes, the less he will have to punish. He must control his temper without however shutting his eyes to faults requiring correction: his instruction must be free from affectation, his industry great, his demands on his class continuous, but not extravagant. He must be ready to answer questions and to put them unmasked to those who sit silent. In praising the recitations of his pupils he must be neither grudging nor over-generous: the former quality will give them a distaste for work, while the latter will produce a complacent self-satisfaction. In correcting faults he must avoid sarcasm and above all abuse:[11] for teachers whose rebukes seem to imply positive dislike discourage industry. He should declaim daily himself and, what is more, without stint, that his class may take his utterances home with them. For however many models for imitation he may give them from the authors they are reading, it will still be found that fuller nourish-

---

11. Among the flaws that appear here and there among teachers "sarcasm and abuse in correcting faults" are among the most damnable. It would seem that Quintilian's humane point would be too obvious to require further emphasis, had one not known of actual occurrences and their unlovely effects. Cp. II.iv.10-12 below.

ment is provided by the living voice, as we call it, more especially when it proceeds from the teacher himself, who, if his pupils are rightly instructed, should be the object of their affection and respect. And it is scarcely possible to say how much more readily we imitate those whom we like.

ii.9-15. Quintilian condemns the practice and evils of indiscriminate applause and warns the teacher to protect the boys against corruption.

I strongly disapprove of the prevailing practice of allowing boys to stand up or leap from the seats in the expression of their applause. Young men, even when they are listening to others, should be temperate in manifesting their approval. If this be insisted upon, the pupil will depend on his instructor's verdict and will take his approval as a guarantee that he has spoken well. The worst form of politeness, as it has come to be called, is that of mutual and indiscriminate applause,[12] a practice which is unseemly, theatrical and unworthy of a decently disciplined school, in addition to being the worst foe to genuine study. For if every effusion is greeted with a storm of ready-made applause, care and industry come to be regarded as superfluous. The audience no less than the speaker should therefore keep their eyes fixed on their teacher's face, since thus they will learn to distinguish between what is praiseworthy and what is not: for just as writing gives facility, so listening begets the critical faculty. But in the schools of to-day we see boys stooping forward ready to spring to their feet: at the close of each period they not merely rise, but rush forward with shouts of unseemly enthusiasm. Such compliments are mutual and the success of a declamation consists in this kind of applause. The result is vanity and empty self-sufficiency, carried to such an extent that, intoxicated by the wild enthusiasm of their fellow-pupils, they conceive a spite against their master, if his praise does not come up to their expectation. But teachers must also insist on receiving an attentive and quiet hearing from the class when they themselves declaim. For the master should not speak to suit his pupils' standard, but they should speak to suit

---

12. Quintilian frequently protests against the sham and hypocrisy of the times and the inordinate passion for approval and praise. Cp. the extravagant superlatives and applause given to mediocre performances on some of our TV talk shows and others today. If every adjective (e.g., "perfectly marvelous") and all applause is undiscriminatingly fortissimo, what is left for true excellence?

(Higher Education) Bk. II.ii, iii

his.¹³ Further he should, if possible, keep his eyes open to note the points which each boy praises and observe the manner in which he expresses his approval, and should rejoice that his words give pleasure not only for his own sake, but for that of those who show sound judgment in their appreciation.

I do not approve of boys sitting mixed with young men. For even if the teacher be such an one as we should desire to see in charge of the morals and studies of the young, and can keep his youthful pupils under proper control, it is none the less desirable to keep the weaker members separate from the more mature, and to avoid not only the actual charge of corruption but the merest suspicion of it. I have thought it worth while to put my views on this subject quite briefly. For I do not think it necessary even to warn the teacher that both he and his school must be free from the grosser vices.¹⁴ And should there be any father who does not trouble to choose a teacher for his son who is free from the obvious taint of immorality, he may rest assured that all the other precepts, which I am attempting to lay down for the benefit of our youth, will be absolutely useless to him, if he neglects this.

iii.1-6. The paramount importance of avoiding inferior teachers of rhetoric and securing the best possible teachers at the very outset even in the elementary stages, for the task of unteaching engrained faults is harder than teaching properly in the first place. The gifted teacher should be willing to address himself to the more elementary details; if not, he is unworthy of the name of teacher. The most capable is the most efficient.

I do not think that I should pass by in silence even the opinion of those who, even when they regard boys as ripe for the rhetorician, still do not think that they should at once be placed under the most eminent teacher available, but prefer to keep them for a while under inferior masters, on the ground that in the elementary stages a mediocre instructor is easier to understand and to

---

13. It would seem very reasonable to agree with Quintilian that the experienced and conscientious teacher—and not the student!—should set the standards of academic performance. And yet we have recently seen callow, aberrant, militant students demanding to impose their dictates even on private educational institutions and the courses and the teachers. "Young people are so busy trying to teach the older people that they have no time to learn anything themselves," says Eric Hoffer. Reasonable educational ferment can be good, but uncontrolled extremes are almost sure to prove disastrous.

14. Cp. note 10 above on II.ii.1.

imitate, and less reluctant to undertake the tiresome task[15] of teaching the rudiments as being beneath his notice. I do not think that I need waste much time in pointing out how much better it is to absorb the best possible principles, or how hard it is to get rid of faults which have once become engrained; for it places a double burden on the shoulders of the later teacher and the preliminary task of unteaching is harder than that of teaching.[16] It is for this reason that the famous piper Timotheus is said to have demanded from those who had previously been under another master a fee double the amount which he charged for those who came to him untaught. The mistake to which I am referring is, however, twofold. First they regard these inferior teachers as adequate for the time being and are content with their instruction because they have a stomach that will swallow anything: this difference, though blameworthy in itself, would yet be tolerable, if the teaching provided by these persons were merely less in quantity and not inferior in quality as well. Secondly, and this is a still commoner delusion, they think that those who are blest with greater gifts of speaking will not condescend to the more elementary details,[17] and that consequently they sometimes disdain to give attention to such inferior subjects of study and sometimes are incapable of so doing. For my part I regard the teacher who is unwilling to attend to such details as being unworthy of the name of teacher: and as for the question of capacity, I maintain that it is the most capable man who, given the will, is able to do this with most efficiency. For in the first place it is a reasonable inference that a man blest with abnormal powers of eloquence will have

15. Note that there has always been a certain amount of tiresome drudgery in teaching and always will be. The teacher-in-training should be advised to face this fact and should resolve to accept it dutifully.

16. It is notorious that the college teachers of English, Latin, and many other subjects find that they often have not only to review but even to reteach the work of earlier teachers at least partly because those earlier teachers were of limited experience and did not require honest and accurate performance from their pupils all the way from the very beginning; and, as Quintilian so rightly observes, the task of unteaching or reteaching is harder than teaching the untaught. Therefore it is a disservice, an unkindness, for the earlier teachers in any institution or system to be too lax in their standards, too easy on their pupils because of their own laziness or fear or a specious attempt to be popular.

17. There has been in some institutions, at least, a tradition that the beginning courses in Latin and Greek should be taught by the older and more seasoned instructors since they can explain the details more clearly and sympathetically. No doubt, however, some scholars are not temperamentally adapted to such work.

(Higher Education) Bk. II.iii

made careful note of the various steps by which eloquence is attained, and in the second place the reasoning faculty, which is specially developed in learned men, is all-important in teaching, while finally no one is eminent in the greater things of his art if he be lacking in the lesser. Unless indeed we are asked to believe that while Phidias modelled his Jupiter to perfection, the decorative details of the statue would have been better executed by another artist, or that an orator does not know how to speak, or a distinguished physician is incapable of treating minor ailments.

iii.7-12. To be sure, the undeveloped boy cannot at the outset comprehend the entirety of a good teacher's knowledge and power of eloquence, but the good teacher must be a sensible man who will adapt himself to his pupil's pace; and the more learned the teacher the more lucid and intelligible is his instruction. Clearness is the first virtue of eloquence; the worse the teacher is, the harder he will be to understand. Not only will a first rate teacher provide better training, but he will also correct errors promptly. The incompetent teacher is more likely to let errors pass without correction.

"Yes" it may be answered "but surely you do not deny that there is a type of eloquence that is too great to be comprehended by undeveloped boys?" Of course there is. But this eloquent teacher whom they fling in my face must be a sensible man with a good knowledge of teaching and must be prepared to stoop to his pupil's level, just as a rapid walker, if walking with a small child, will give him his hand and lessen his own speed and avoid advancing at a pace beyond the powers of his little companion. Again it frequently happens that the more learned the teacher, the more lucid and intelligible is his instruction. For clearness[18] is the first virtue of eloquence, and the less talented a man is, the more he will strive to exalt and dilate himself, just as short men tend to walk on tip-toe and weak men to use threats. As for those whose style is inflated or vicious, and whose language reveals a passion for high-sounding words or labours under any other form of

18. Clearness is a paramount virtue for any teacher and any other person who aspires to any effectiveness among his fellow men. This implies the ability to express oneself accurately and effectively, which in turn makes the careful study of languages (at least one's mother tongue) an obvious necessity. To the Romans this justified their extensive study of language, literature, composition, and rhetoric. Today's slovenly speaking and writing habits bear witness to the dire need of such discipline for us. Let the teacher of any subject unremittingly require clear and accurate expression from his students at all times, and let the teacher himself set the example. "The worse a teacher is the harder he will be to understand." Cp. IV.ii.36,39; VIII.ii.22-23.

affectation, in my opinion they suffer not from excess of strength but of weakness, like bodies swollen not with the plumpness of health but with disease, or like men who weary of the direct road betake them to bypaths. Consequently the worse a teacher is, the harder he will be to understand.

I have not forgotten that I stated in the preceding book, when I urged that school was preferable to home education, that pupils at the commencement of their studies, when progress is as yet but in the bud, are more disposed to imitate their schoolfellows than their masters, since such imitation comes more easily to them. Some of my readers may think that the view which I am now maintaining is inconsistent with my previous statement. But I am far from being inconsistent: for my previous assertion affords the strongest reason for selecting the very best teachers for our boys; since pupils of a first rate master, having received a better training, will when they speak say something that may be worthy of imitation, while if they commit some mistake, they will be promptly corrected.[19] But the incompetent teacher on the other hand is quite likely to give his approval to faulty work and by the judgment which he expresses to force approval on the audience. The teacher should therefore be as distinguished for his eloquence as for his good character, and like Phoenix in the *Iliad* be able to teach his pupil both how to behave and how to speak.[20]

iv.1-8. Elementary rhetorical exercises. Narrative, three kinds: (1) fictitious as in tragedies and poems; (2) realistic as in comedies; (3) historical or actual fact. In style the extremes of too dry and too fanciful (poetic license) are to be avoided; but it is better for a boy to err in the direction of exuberance than of barrenness since in time reason will file away many excrescences.

I shall now proceed to indicate what I think should be the first subjects in which the rhetorician should give instruction, and shall postpone for a time our consideration of the art of rhetoric

---

19. Another important pedagogical technique, as valid for us as for Quintilian, is the *immediate* correction of errors when they occur, before they have a chance to pile up in a bewildering tangled mess. Prompt correction keeps students accurately up-to-date; lax remissness is, sad to say, too common and leads to misery. Cp. also I.i.11.

20. Phoenix went to Troy as the tutor of Achilles. In Homer's *Iliad,* IX.443, Phoenix says that he was sent to teach Achilles how "to be both a speaker of words and a doer of deeds." This is one of the earliest recorded statements of the purpose of education; and it emphasizes the importance of speech.

(Higher Education) Bk. II.iii, iv

in the narrow sense in which that term is popularly used. For in my opinion it is most desirable that we should commence with something resembling the subjects already acquired under the teacher of literature.

Now there are three forms of narrative, without counting the type used in actual legal cases. First there is the fictitious narrative as we get it in tragedies and poems, which is not merely not true but has little resemblance to truth. Secondly, there is the realistic narrative as presented by comedies, which, though not true, has yet a certain verisimilitude. Thirdly there is the historical narrative, which is an exposition of actual fact. Poetic narratives are the property of the teacher of literature.[21] The rhetorician therefore should begin with the historical narrative, whose force is in proportion to its truth. I will, however, postpone my demonstration of what I regard as the best method of narration till I come to deal with narration as required in the courts. In the meantime, it will be sufficient to urge that it should be neither dry or jejune (for why spend so much labour over our studies if a bald and naked statement of fact is regarded as sufficiently expressive?); nor on the other hand must it be tortuous or revel in elaborate descriptions, such as those in which so many are led to indulge by a misguided imitation of poetic licence. Both these extremes are faults;[22] but that which springs from poverty of wit is worse than that which is due to imaginative excess.[23] For we cannot demand or expect a perfect style from boys. But there is greater promise in a certain luxuriance of mind, in ambitious effort and an ardour that leads at times to ideas bordering on the extravagant. I have no objection to a little exuberance in the young learner. Nay, I would urge teachers too like nurses to be careful to provide softer food for still undeveloped minds and to suffer them to take their fill of the milk of the more attractive studies. For the time being the body may be somewhat plump, but maturer years will reduce it to a sparer habit. Such plumpness gives hopes of strength; a child fully formed in every limb is likely to grow up a puny

---

21. I.e., the *grammaticus.*
22. Here, as so often, Quintilian proclaims the wise classical doctrine of *sophrosyne,* moderation: that the best regularly lies between the extremes of too little and too much. Horace's famous term is *aurea mediocritas,* the "golden mean."
23. Quintilian's actual word is *copia,* "abundance; richness of expression," which is a term commonly used to characterize the style of Cicero, who was Quintilian's great exemplar.

weakling. The young should be more daring and inventive and should rejoice in their inventions, even though correctness and severity are still to be acquired. Exuberance is easily remedied, but barrenness is incurable, be your efforts what they may. To my mind the boy who gives least promise is one in whom the critical faculty develops in advance of the imagination. I like to see the first fruits of the mind copious to excess and almost extravagant in their profusion. The years as they pass will skim off much of the froth, reason will file away[24] many excrescences, and something too will be removed by what I may perhaps call the wear and tear of life, so long as there is sufficient material to admit of cutting and chiselling away. And there will be sufficient, if only we do not draw the plate too thin to begin with, so that it runs the risk of being broken if the graver cut too deep. Those of my readers who know their Cicero will not be surprised that I take this view: for does he not say "I would have the youthful mind run riot in the luxuriance of its growth"?

iv.8-14. Digression about the teacher. Especial care must be taken to avoid a dry *teacher! For such a teacher will stunt a boy's academic growth. In correcting faults a teacher should not be so severe as to discourage a boy's mind. Rather he should be as kindly as possible and should* give reasons *for any necessary alterations in the boy's work. Quintilian's own firm but gentle methods cited from his own experience.*

We must, therefore, take especial care, above all where boys are concerned, to avoid a dry[25] teacher, even as we avoid a dry and arid soil for plants that are still young and tender. For with such a teacher their growth is stunted and their eyes are turned earthwards, and they are afraid to rise above the level of daily speech. Their leanness is regarded as a sign of health and their weakness as a sign of sound judgment, and while they are content that their work should be devoid of faults they fall into the fault of being devoid of merit. So let not the ripeness of vintage come too soon nor the must turn harsh while yet in the vat; thus it will last for years and mellow with age.

24. Quintilian's *limabit* suggests Horace's *labor limae,* "the labor of the file," which picturesquely portrays the process through which a composition is perfected by reworking and polishing, by "filing."

25. It is said that one of the best means of motivating students is the contagious enthusiasm of the teacher. Where a teacher is dry, unimaginative, uninterested and uninteresting, the situation can hardly be joyously productive. Cp. also Quintilian's comment on *dry* textbooks in Book I, Preface §24 and note 7 thereon.

(Higher Education) Bk. II.iv

10 It is worth while too to warn the teacher that undue severity in correcting[26] faults is liable at times to discourage a boy's mind from effort. He loses hope and gives way to vexation, then last of all comes to hate his work and fearing everything attempts nothing. 11 This phenomenon is familiar to farmers, who hold that the pruning-hook should not be applied while the leaves are yet young, for they seem to "shrink from the steel" and to be unable as yet to endure a scar. 12 The instructor therefore should be as kindly as possible at this stage; remedies, which are harsh by nature, must be applied with a gentle hand: some portions of the work must be praised, others tolerated and others altered: the reason for the alterations should however be given,[27] and in some cases the master will illumine an obscure passage by inserting something of his own. Occasionally again the teacher will find it useful to dictate whole themes himself that the boy may imitate them and for the time being love them as if they were his own. 13 But if a boy's composition is so careless as not to admit of correction, I have found[28] it useful to give a fresh exposition of the theme and tell him to write it again, pointing out that he was capable of doing better: for there is nothing like hope for making study a pleasure. 14 Different ages however demand different methods: the task set and the standard of correction must be proportioned to the pupil's strength. When boys ventured on something that was too daring or exuberant, I used to say to them that I approved of it for the moment, but that the time would come when I could no longer tolerate such a style. The result was that the consciousness of ability filled them with pleasure, without blinding their judgment.

iv.15-17. To continue, written narratives should be composed with utmost care. Similarly in speaking, boys should not be permitted to indulge in extempore and undisciplined effusions and ostentatious displays which develop arrogant but empty convictions of their own talents. Only by dint of taking pains and working hard are they likely to produce

---

26. On this same manner of correcting see II.ii.7 and note 11 above.
27. Here, as throughout this passage, Quintilian is to be blessed for his humanity—and is to be imitated. Too often people seek to correct and rule by arbitrary fiat rather than by giving reasons.
28. This passage provides a particularly clear and attractive vignette of the master teacher Quintilian at work, speaking propria persona out of his own experience and practice (though of course he does so constantly).

something worthy of approval. Let them learn to speak correctly before they try to speak rapidly.

However, to return to the point from which I had digressed. Written narratives should be composed with the utmost care. It is useful at first, when a child has just begun to speak, to make him repeat what he has heard with a view to improving his powers of speech; and for the same purpose, and with good reason, I would make him tell his story from the end back to the beginning or start in the middle and go backwards or forwards, but only so long as he is at his teacher's knee and while he is incapable of greater effort and is beginning to connect words and things, thereby strengthening the memory. Even so when he is beginning to understand the nature of correct and accurate speech, extempore effusions, improvised without waiting for thought to supply the matter or a moment's hesitation before rising to the feet, must not be permitted: they proceed from a passion for display that would do credit to a common mountebank. Such proceedings fill ignorant parents with senseless pride, while the boys themselves lose all respect for their work, adopt a conceited bearing, and acquire the habit of speaking in the worst style and actually practising their faults, while they develop an arrogant conviction of their own talents which often proves fatal even to the most genuine proficiency. There will be a special time for acquiring fluency in speech and I shall not pass the subject by unnoticed. For the meantime it will suffice if a boy, by dint of taking pains and working as hard as age will permit, manages to produce something worthy of approval. Let him get used to this until it becomes a second nature. It is only he who learns to speak correctly before he can speak with rapidity[29] who will reach the heights that are our goal or the levels immediately below them.

iv.20-25. Other topics for rhetorical exercises: praise, denunciation, comparison of two characters, commonplaces, theses.

From this our pupil will begin to proceed to more important themes, such as the praise of famous men and the denunciation of the wicked. Such tasks are profitable in more than one respect. The mind is exercised by the variety and multiplicity of the subject matter, while the character is moulded by the contemplation of virtue and vice. Further wide knowledge of facts is thus acquired, from which examples may be drawn if circumstances so

29. Again, *festina lente* (see I.i.32 and note 15 thereon).

demand, such illustrations being of the utmost value in every kind of case. It is but a step from this to practice in the comparison of the respective merits of two characters. This is of course a very similar theme to the preceding, but involves a duplication of the subject matter and deals not merely with the nature of virtues and vices, but with their degree as well. But the method to be followed in panegyric and invective will be dealt with in its proper place, as it forms the third department of rhetoric.

As to *commonplaces* (I refer to those in which we denounce vices themselves such as adultery, gambling or profligacy without attacking particular persons), they come straight from the courts and, if we add the name of the defendant, amount to actual accusations. As a rule, however, the general character of a commonplace is usually given a special turn: for instance we make our adulterer blind, our gambler poor and our profligate far advanced in years. Sometimes too they entail defence: for we may speak on behalf of luxury or love, while a pimp or a parasite may be defended in such a way that we appear as counsel not for the character itself, but to rebut some specific charge that is brought against him.

Theses on the other hand are concerned with the comparison of things and involve questions such as "Which is preferable, town or country life?" or "Which deserves the greatest[30] praise, the lawyer or the soldier?" These provide the most attractive and copious practice in the art of speaking, and are most useful whether we have an eye to the duties of deliberative oratory or the arguments of the courts. For instance Cicero in his *pro Murena*[31] deals very fully with the second of the two problems mentioned above. Other *theses* too belong entirely to the deliberative class of oratory, as for instance the question as to "Whether marriage is desirable" or "Whether a public career is a proper object of ambition." Put such discussions into the mouths of specific persons and they become deliberative declamations at once.

v.1-9. Assistance to be given to students. The nature and value of the classroom technique of explication of texts by explanatory lecturing. Note that the pupils are to be actively involved in the process.

I will speak of the theory of declamation a little later. In the

---

30. Since only two people are involved here, strictly correct syntax requires not "greatest" but "greater," which is exactly what Quintilian's Latin has (i.e., *maior*).

31. *Pro Murena* IX.21 ff.

meantime, as we are discussing the elementary stages of a rhetorical education, I think I should not fail to point out how greatly the rhetorician will contribute to his pupils' progress, if he imitates the teacher of literature whose duty it is to expound the poets,[32] and gives the pupils whom he has undertaken to train, instruction in the reading of history and still more of the orators. I myself have adopted this practice for the benefit of a few pupils of suitable age whose parents thought it would be useful. But though my intentions were excellent, I found that there were two serious obstacles to success: long custom had established a different method of teaching, and my pupils were for the most part full-grown youths who did not require this form of teaching, but were taking my work as their model. However, the fact that I have been somewhat late in making the discovery is not a reason why I should be ashamed to recommend it to those who come after me.[33] I now know that this form of teaching is practised by the Greeks, but is generally entrusted to assistants, as the professors themselves consider that they have no time to give individual instruction to each pupil as he reads. And I admit that the form of lecture[34] which this requires, designed as it is to make boys follow the written word with ease and accuracy, and even that which aims at teaching the meaning of any rare words that may occur, are to be regarded as quite below the dignity of the teacher of rhetoric. On the other hand it is emphatically part of his profession and the undertaking which he makes in offering himself as a teacher of eloquence, to point out the merits of authors or, for that matter, any faults that may occur: and this is all the more the case, as I am not asking teachers to undertake the task of recalling their pupils to stand at their knee once more and of assisting them in the reading of whatever book they may select. It seems to me at

32. For instance, see Book I.viii.13-15,17-18 regarding the nature of the lectures of the grammaticus. The rhetor, however, will naturally prefer history and speeches as more appropriate subjects for his explicatory lectures in the field of oratory.

33. Note Quintilian's open-mindedness and candor in recommending a good technique which he himself was actually late in discovering.

34. This form of lecture described in §§5-9 below we may call explication of the text. It is a classroom technique as valid for us today as for Quintilian, especially in such courses as language and literature. Note, however, that it is not quite the same thing as the enormous "lecture courses" which have lately come under attack for their size and impersonality.

(Higher Education) Bk. II.v

once an easier and more profitable method to call for silence and choose some one pupil—and it will be best to select them by turns—to read aloud, in order that they may at the same time learn the correct method of elocution.[35] The case with which the speech selected for reading is concerned should then be explained, for if this be done they will have a clearer understanding of what is to be read. When the reading is commenced, no important point should be allowed to pass unnoticed either as regards the resourcefulness or the style shown in the treatment of the subject: the teacher must point out how the orator seeks to win the favour of the judge in his *exordium*,[36] what clearness, brevity and sincerity, and at times what shrewd design and well-concealed artifice is shown in the statement of facts. For the only true art in pleading is that which can only be understood by one who is a master of the art himself. The teacher will proceed further to demonstrate what skill is shown in the division into heads, how subtle and frequent are the thrusts of argument, what vigour marks the stirring and what charm the soothing passage, how fierce is the invective and how full of wit the jests, and in conclusion how the orator establishes his sway over the emotions of his audience, forces his way into their very hearts and brings the feelings of the jury into perfect sympathy with all his words. Finally as regards the style, he will emphasise the appropriateness, elegance or sublimity of particular words, will indicate where the amplification of the theme is deserving of praise and where there is virtue in a diminuendo; and will call attention to brilliant metaphors, figures of speech and passages combining smoothness and polish with a general impression of manly vigour.

v.10-12. Even bad speeches can be thus treated advantageously to show how many expressions in them are inappropriate, obscure, high-flown, low, vile, or extravagant—even though they are praised by most people since that which is abnormal is admired as exquisite.

It will even at times be of value to read speeches which are

---

35. Quintilian's suggestion to involve students in this exercise is an excellent one well worth our adoption whenever and however possible. Involvement of this sort makes for good motivation, attention, and the personal satisfaction which comes from participation. Also cp. §13 below.

36. *Exordium*, the Latin word for the introductory part of a speech, has been taken over into English without any change.

corrupt and faulty in style, but still meet with general admiration thanks to the perversity of modern tastes,[37] and to point out how many expressions in them are inappropriate, obscure, highflown, grovelling, mean, extravagant or effeminate, although they are not merely praised by the majority of critics, but, worse still, praised just because they are bad. For we have come to regard direct and natural speech as incompatible with genius, while all that is in any way abnormal is admired as exquisite. Similarly we see that some people place a higher value on figures which are in any way monstrous or distorted than they do on those who have not lost any of the advantages of the normal form of man. There are even some who are captivated by the shams of artifice and think that there is more beauty in those who pluck out superfluous hair or use depilatories, who dress their locks by scorching them with the curling iron and glow with a complexion that is not their own, than can ever be conferred by nature pure and simple, so that it really seems as if physical beauty depended entirely on moral hideousness.[38]

v.13-17. It is also the duty of the instructor to ask frequent questions and test the critical powers of the students. This will help the class to keep alert and encourage them to become self-reliant. Practice is more valuable than precept.

It will, however, be the duty of the rhetorician not merely to teach these things, but to ask frequent questions[39] as well, and test the critical powers of his class. This will prevent his audience from becoming inattentive and will secure that his words do not fall on deaf ears. At the same time the class will be led to find out things for themselves and to use their intelligence, which is after all the chief aim of this method of training. For what else is our object in teaching, save that our pupils should not always require to be

37. Once again we can hardly fail to notice the unfortunate similarity of our own times as, for example, in certain kinds of programs when undiscriminating audiences applaud stupid, inane, substandard, ignorant, barbaric language as loudly as they do good, decent, effective, standard, and even elegant language.

38. If Quintilian indicts the sham and speciousness of his own times thus, what would he say of the signs of decadence in our times! The question of values is ever old and ever new, ever difficult and ever of prime concern. What are decent, worthwhile values and who is to inculcate them?

39. It is interesting to see that the frequent asking of questions is an old and well-tested method of encouraging student participation. Although the results can often be frustrating and exasperating, this technique because of its values here set forth by Quintilian must never be abandoned.

(Higher Education) Bk. II.v

taught? I will venture to say that this particular form of exercise, if diligently pursued, will teach learners more than all the textbooks of all the rhetoricians: these are no doubt of very considerable use, but being somewhat general in their scope, it is quite impossible for them to deal with all the special cases that are of almost daily occurrence. The art of war will provide a parallel: it is no doubt based on certain general principles, but it will none the less be far more useful to know the methods employed, whether wisely or the reverse, by individual generals under varying circumstances and conditions of time and place. For there are no subjects in which, as a rule, practice is not more valuable than precept. Is a teacher to declaim to provide a model for his audience, and will not more profit be derived from the reading of Cicero or Demosthenes? Is a pupil to be publicly corrected if he makes a mistake in declaiming, and will it not be more useful, and more agreeable too, to correct some actual speech? For everyone has a preference for hearing the faults of others censured rather than his own. I might say more on the subject. But everyone can see the advantages of this method. Would that the reluctance to put it into practice were not as great as the pleasure that would undoubtedly be derived from so doing!

v.18-26. What authors should be read at this stage? From the very beginning read only the best, choosing the simplest and most intelligible at first; e.g., Livy and Cicero. Avoid extremes, especially of the current florid school.

This method once adopted, we are faced by the comparatively easy question as to what authors should be selected for our reading. Some have recommended authors of inferior merit on the ground that they were easier to understand. Others on the contrary would select the more florid school of writers on the ground that they are likely to provide the nourishment best suited to the minds of the young. For my part I would have them read the best authors from the very beginning and never leave them, choosing those, however, who are simplest and most intelligible. For instance, when prescribing for boys, I should give Livy[40] the preference over Sallust: for, although the latter is the greater

---

40. Livy, who died about eighteen years before the birth of Quintilian, wrote the most famous and most colorful history of Rome from the founding of the city down to his own times. Very many of the vivid stories which we associate with Rome derive from his history. Livy's "painted page" lives today, whereas Sallust's work is known chiefly to scholars.

historian, one requires to be well-advanced in one's studies to appreciate him properly. Cicero, in my opinion, provides pleasant reading for beginners and is sufficiently easy to understand: it is possible not only to learn much from him, but to come to love him.[41] After Cicero, I should, following the advice of Livy, place such authors as most nearly resemble him.

There are two faults of taste against which boys should be guarded with the utmost care. Firstly no teacher suffering from an excessive admiration of antiquity, should be allowed to cramp their minds by the study of Cato and the Gracchi[42] and other similar authors. For such reading will give them a harsh and bloodless style, since they will as yet be unable to understand the force and vigour of these authors, and contenting themselves with a style which doubtless was admirable in its day, but is quite unsuitable to ours, will come to think (and nothing could be more fatal) that they really resemble great men. Secondly the opposite extreme must be equally avoided: they must not be permitted to fall victims to the pernicious allurements of the precious blooms produced by our modern euphuists,[43] thus acquiring a passion for the luscious sweetness of such authors, whose charm is all the more attractive to boyish intellects because it is so easy of achievement. Once, however, the judgment is formed and out of danger of perversion, I should strongly recommend the reading of ancient authors, since if, after clearing away all the uncouthness of those rude ages, we succeed in absorbing the robust vigour and virility of their native genius, our more finished style will shine with an added grace: I also approve the study of the moderns at this stage, since even they have many merits. For nature has not doomed us to be dullards, but we have altered our style of oratory and indulged our caprices over much. It is their ideals rather than their talents that the ancients show themselves our superiors. It will therefore be possible to select much that is valuable from modern writers, but we must take care that the

41. This fine tribute to Cicero reflects Quintilian's oft-expressed respect and fondness for Cicero.
42. Cato and the two Gracchi were famous figures in the second century B.C. some two hundred years before Quintilian's time.
43. I.e., the florid school (see §18 above) that blossomed in the first century of our era. It was characterized by extravagant style, poetic flavor, effusiveness, artificiality, preciousness, a passion for epigrammatic point to the extent that clever and brilliant form often seemed more important than substance.

precious metal is not debased by the dross with which it is so closely intermingled. Further I would not merely gladly admit, but would even contend that we have recently had and still have certain authors who deserve imitation in their entirety. But it is not for everyone to decide who these writers are. Error in the choice of earlier authors is attended with less danger, and I have therefore postponed the study of the moderns, for fear that we should imitate them before we are qualified to judge of their merits.

vi.1-7. The composition of declamations—two methods of teaching: (1) give pupils complete exemplars for their themes, (2) provide a bare outline followed by criticism of errors. It is best to employ both methods conjointly, allowing for some variation.

I come now to another point in which the practice of teachers has differed. Some have not been content with giving directions as to the arrangement of the subjects set them as themes for declamation, but have developed them at some length themselves, supplying not merely the proofs, but the lines upon which the emotional passages should proceed. Others have merely suggested a bare outline, and then when the declamations were over, have indicated the points missed by each speaker and worked up certain passages with no less care than they would have used, had they been going to stand up to speak themselves. Both practices have their advantages, and therefore I will not give either the pre-eminence. But if we must choose one of the two, it will be found more profitable to point out the right road at the onset, and not merely to recall the pupil from his error when he had already gone astray, since in the first place the correction is only received by the ear, whereas when he is given a sketch of the various heads of the declamation, he has to take them down and think about them: secondly instruction is always more readily received than reproof. Indeed those of our pupils who have a lively disposition are liable in the present condition of manners to lose their temper when admonished and to offer silent resistance.[44] That, however, is no reason for refraining from the public correction of faults; for we must take the rest of the class into account, who will believe that whatever has not been cor-

---

44. It is hardly surprising to find that the ancient Roman pupils were not unlike their counterparts today. From this and other observations it seems that human nature has changed little in two thousand years.

rected by the master is right. The two methods should be employed conjointly and in such a way as circumstances may demand. Beginners must be given a subject sketched out ready for treatment and suitable to their respective powers. But when they show that they have formed themselves sufficiently closely on the models placed before them, it will be sufficient to give them a few brief hints for their guidance and to allow them to advance trusting in their own strength and without external support. Sometimes they should be left entirely to their own devices, that they may not be spoilt by the bad habit of always relying on another's effort, and so prove incapable of effort and originality. But as soon as they seem to have acquired a sound conception of what they ought to say, the teacher's work will be near completion: if they still make some mistakes, they must be brought back under his guidance. We may draw a lesson from the birds of the air, whom we see distributing the food which they have collected in their bills among their weak and helpless nestlings; but as soon as they are fledged, we see them teaching their young to leave the nest and fly round about it, themselves leading the way; finally, when they have proved their strength, they are given the freedom of the open sky and left to trust in themselves.

vii.1-5. Memorization. The common practice of having pupils memorize and declaim all their compositions is to be discouraged. Boys should spend as much time as possible over their written compositions; but they should memorize for declamation passages selected from recognized orators, historians, and the like. The great benefits accruing from memorization are praised. Occasionally a pupil may be permitted to declaim one of his own compositions which is more polished than usual.

There is one practice at present in vogue for boys of the age under discussion, which ought in my opinion undoubtedly to be changed. They should not be forced to commit all their own compositions to memory and to deliver them on an appointed day, as is at present the custom. This practice is especially popular with the boys' fathers,[45] who think that their sons are not really

---

45. There have always been parents who have been more interested, perhaps selfishly, in their children's showy declamations than they have been concerned to encourage that industry which is requisite for real progress. To be sure, boys should declaim their own composition occasionally but only when they have produced something extraordinarily good, something excellent, which merits praise (see §5 below). Is it wrong to provide motivation for excellence?

(Higher Education) Bk. II.vi, vii

studying unless they declaim on every possible occasion, although as a matter of fact progress depends mainly on industry. For though I strongly approve of boys writing compositions and would have them spend as much time as possible over such tasks, I had much rather that for the purpose of learning by heart[46] passages should be selected from the orators or historians or any other works that may be deserving of attention. For it is a better exercise for the memory to learn the words of others than it is to learn one's own, and those who have practised this far harder task will find no difficulty in committing to memory their own compositions with which they are already familiar. Further they will form an intimate acquaintance with the best writings, will carry their models with them and unconsciously reproduce the style of the speech which has been impressed upon the memory. They will have a plentiful and choice vocabulary and a command of artistic structure and a supply of figures which will not have to be hunted for, but will offer themselves spontaneously from the treasure-house, if I may so call it, in which they are stored. In addition they will be in the agreeable position of being able to quote the happy sayings of the various authors, a power which they will find most useful in the courts. For phrases which have not been coined merely to suit the circumstances of the lawsuit of the moment carry greater weight and often win greater praise than if they were our own. I would however allow boys occasion-

---

46. This passage (§§2-4) is a fine little essay on the values of the memorization of judiciously chosen material especially when one is young and the powers of memory are at their peak. These values are still attested by many who were educated in our older curriculum, where memorization played such a beneficial role. For example, what a source of comfort, strength, and inspiration it is for people of all ages to be able to recall from memory at any place and any time something like the Lord's Prayer or the Twenty-Third Psalm. If one multiplies great passages like these many, many times over, one comes to have the well-stocked treasure-house (thesaurus) mentioned in §4 on which to draw rich dividends throughout life (cp. I.i.36 above); and, of course, there are similar applications of memory in the realm of facts, such as $7 \times 9 = 63$. However, new fads have come in according to which memorization along with "sin" and "discipline" are to be eliminated from our educational thinking and programming as unpleasant, wearisome, harrassing concepts and possibly dangerous to the extent that they might cause some sort of psychological disturbance or complex if one were required to face up to them. Let us hope that the pendulum will swing back to the midground of sanity. Cp. excerpts from Book XI below concerning memory. Memory and reason are different and accomplish different things; we should train and cultivate both.

ally to declaim their own compositions that they may reap the reward of their labours in the applause of a large audience, that most coveted of all prizes. But this should not be permitted until they have produced something more finished than usual: they will thus be rewarded for their industry and rejoice in the thought that the privilege accorded them is the recompense of merit.

viii.1-15. Different pupils require different methods. Many people think that the rhetor should push the pupil forward chiefly in the field of his special talents. The rhetor will distinguish special aptitudes, to be sure; but a candidate for the bar must perfect himself in all the accomplishments required by his profession, even though some subjects may seem too hard for him at first. Defects must be made good and weaknesses made strong so far as it is at all possible.

It is generally and not unreasonably regarded as the sign of a good teacher that he should be able to differentiate between the abilities of his respective pupils and to know their natural bent.[47] The gifts of nature are infinite in their variety, and mind differs from mind almost as much as body from body. This is clear from a consideration of the orators themselves, who differ in style to such an extent that no one is like another, in spite of the fact that numbers have modelled their style on that of their favorite authors. Many again think it useful to direct their instruction to the fostering of natural advantages and to guide the talents of their pupils along the lines which they instinctively tend to follow. Just as an expert gymnast, when he enters a gymnasium full of boys, after testing body and mind in every way, is able to decide for what class of athletic contest they should be trained, even so, they say, a teacher of oratory after careful observation of a boy's stylistic preferences, be they for terseness and polish, energy, dignity, charm, roughness, brilliance or wit, will so adapt his instructions to individual needs that each pupil will be pushed forward in the sphere for which his talents seem specially to design him;[48] for nature, when cultivated, goes from strength to

---

47. Again Quintilian says that the good teacher will seek to assess the abilities of his pupils; cp. I.iii.1. This indicates teacher concern about pupils.

48. Apparently some educationists of Quintilian's time would agree with some moderns that a pupil should not be required to conform to any definite curriculum but should be free to do what he pleases according to his natural bents. This theory is entertained by not a few parents as well, who say: "If my son is interested only in commercial art [for instance], why should he be required to waste any time on literature, language, history, mathematics, etc.?" This thought

strength, while he who runs counter to her bent is ineffective in those branches of the art for which he is less suited and weakens the talents which he seemed born to employ.

Now, since the critic who is guided by his reason is free to dissent even from received opinions, I must insist that to my thinking this view is only partially true. It is undoubtedly necessary to note the individual gifts of each boy, and no one would ever convince me that it is not desirable to differentiate courses of study with this in view. One boy will be better adapted for the study of history, another for poetry, another for law, while some perhaps had better be packed off to the country.[49] The teacher of rhetoric will distinguish such special aptitudes, just as our gymnast will turn one pupil into a runner, another into a boxer or wrestler or an expert at some other of the athletic accomplishments for which prizes are awarded at the sacred games.

But on the other hand, he who is destined for the bar must study not one department merely, but must perfect himself in all the accomplishments which his profession demands, even though some of them may seem too hard for him when he approaches them as a learner.[50] For if natural talent alone were sufficient, education might be dispensed with. Suppose we are given a pupil who, like so many, is of depraved tastes and swollen with his own

has also been recently stressed by students who set themselves up as instantaneous authorities in education and demand the right to revamp the courses and curricula of their educational institutions according to their own wishes. Older people, even though well experienced in education, must show young people the courtesy of listening to and learning from what they have to say. In their turn young people, inexperienced and impetuous as they are bound to be, have no right to claim omniscience and expect their elders to accede to their every request. The whole world needs a sincere attempt at accommodation and reasonableness without the pigheadedness of the placard which read: "Be reasonable; do it my way."

49. Here Quintilian does admit the reasonableness of a certain amount of specialization in accordance with the natural talents of a student. In the case of those of weaker understanding perhaps all they can do is to follow their natural bents (see §§12-13 below) in a limited education, while the words "some had perhaps better be packed off to the country" seem to suggest that not everyone is cut out for college work after all.

50. In this paragraph, however, Quintilian maintains that the highest accomplishments in, and the fullest benefits of, education require a well-rounded educational experience and discipline beyond merely a single department of special interest. We have a fine picture of education at work pruning, enriching, and molding the individual into a greater and stronger person and a richer personality—like a harp with all its strings in tune.

conceit; shall we suffer him to go his own sweet way? If a boy's disposition is naturally dry and jejune, ought we not to feed it up or at any rate clothe it in fairer apparel? For, if in some cases it is necessary to remove certain qualities, surely there are others where we may be permitted to add what is lacking. Not that I would set myself against the will of nature. No innate good quality should be neglected, but defects must be made good and weaknesses made strong. When Isocrates, the prince of instructors, whose works proclaim his eloquence no less than his pupils testify to his excellence as a teacher, gave his opinion of Ephorus and Theopompus to the effect that the former needed the spur and the latter the curb, what was his meaning? Surely not that the sluggish temperament of the one and the headlong ardour of the other alike required modification by instruction, but rather that each would gain from an admixture of the qualities of the other.

In the case of weaker understandings however some concession must be made and they should be directed merely to follow the call of their nature, since thus they will be more effective in doing the only thing that lies in their power. But if we are fortunate enough to meet with richer material, such as justifies us in the hope of producing a real orator, we must leave no oratorical virtue uncared for. For though he will necessarily have a natural bent for some special department of oratory, he will not feel repelled by the others, and by sheer application will develop his other qualities until they equal those in which he naturally excels. The skilled gymnast will once again provide us with a parallel: if he undertakes to train a pancratiast,[51] he will not merely teach him how to use his fists or his heels, nor will he restrict his instructions to the holds in wrestling, giving special attention to certain tricks of this kind, but will train him in every department of the science. Some will no doubt be incapable of attaining proficiency in certain exercises; these must specialize on some which lie within their powers. For there are two things which he must be most careful to avoid: first, he must not attempt the impossible, secondly he must not switch off his pupil from what he can do well to exercises for which he is less well suited. But if his pupil is like the famous Nicostratus, whom we saw when he was old and we were boys, he will train him equally in every depart-

---

51. The pancration was a no-holds-barred contest which combined wrestling, boxing, kicking, gouging, and the like.

(Higher Education) Bk. II.viii, ix, x

ment of the science and will make him a champion both in boxing and wrestling, like Nicostratus himself who won the prize for both contests within a few days of each other. And how much more important is the employment of such methods where our future orator is concerned! It is not enough to be able to speak with terseness, subtlety or vehemence, any more than it would be for a singing master to excel in the upper, middle or lower register alone. Eloquence is like a harp and will never reach perfection, unless all its strings be taut and in tune.

ix.1-3. The perfect student-teacher relationship—concord.

Though I have spoken in some detail of the duties of the teacher, I shall for the moment confine my advice to the learners to one solitary admonition, that they should love their masters not less than their studies,[52] and should regard them as the parents not indeed of their bodies but of their minds. Such attachments are of invaluable assistance to study. For under their influence they find it a pleasure to listen to their teachers, believe what they say and long to be like them, come cheerfully and gladly to school, are not angry when corrected, rejoice when praised, and seek to win their master's affection by the devotion with which they pursue their studies. For as it is the duty of the master to teach, so it is the duty of the pupil to show himself teachable. The two obligations are mutually indispensable. And just as it takes two parents to produce a human being, and as the seed is scattered in vain, if the ground is hard and there is no furrow to receive it and bring it to growth, even so eloquence can never come to maturity, unless teacher and taught are in perfect sympathy.

x.1-15. The theory of declamation on deliberative and forensic themes. However, declamation in actual practice has so degenerated through the fault of our teachers that it has become one of the chief causes of the corruption of modern oratory; such is the extravagance and ignorance of our declaimers. To redeem declamation for its valid use, subjects chosen for themes should be as true to life as possible and modelled on the forensic practice for which it is a training.

These elementary stages[53] are in themselves no small undertak-

52. "My advice to learners . . . that they should love their masters [i.e., teachers] not less than their studies." This would certainly be an ideal situation; but one doubts that teachers can ipso facto *command* students' love. Rather teachers (like anybody else) have to strive to *win* such love—though be it noted that supine permissiveness is the last way to win it.

53. See especially Chapters iv, vi, and vii above.

ing, but they are merely members and portions of the greater whole; when therefore the pupil has been thoroughly instructed and exercised in these departments, the time will as a rule have come for him to attempt deliberative and forensic themes. But before I begin to discuss these, I must say a few words on the theory of declamation, which is at once the most recent and most useful of rhetorical exercises. For it includes practically all the 2 exercises of which we have been speaking and is in close touch with reality. As a result it has acquired such a vogue that many think that it is the sole training necessary to the formation of an orator, since there is no excellence in a formal speech which is not also to be found in this type of rhetorical exercise. On the other 3 hand the actual practice of declamation has degenerated to such an extent owing to the fault of our teachers, that it has come to be one of the chief causes of the corruption of modern oratory;[54]

54. This passage can be best understood through a statement about the need and use of genuine, free, untrammeled oratory in the days of the Roman democracy, roughly, up through the first century B.C. During the republic a free and outspoken oratory was necessary for the conduct of the affairs of a democratic state where the people in assembly and their elected officials and the Senate were the government (Senatus Populusque Romanus). By the aid of this unrestricted oratory officials were elected, laws were proposed and enacted, problems were debated and "settled," great citizens and deeds were praised, cases were conducted in court. In the late Roman republic it was the rhetor, the professor of rhetoric, who provided the training for the clear, effective, persuasive speaking necessary for all such occasions. When democracy finally decayed and died at Rome (let us today also beware!), one-man rule was established. Augustus, the first emperor, was reasonably benign as were some others. Some like Nero and Domitian in Quintilian's time were insufferable and capricious autocrats and paid very scant attention to the Senatus Populusque Romanus. For who would dare to speak out openly against the policies and the officials favored by the imperial rulers? These times, therefore, provided no real public forum for a completely free and democratic oratory. (Compare the plight of free speech in unfree, regimented societies today.) Consequently, the spirit and occasion of the old-time political oratory died under the imperial blight. However, rhetoric, the art of composition and oratory, continued to keep its hold on Roman education; but now too often the professors of rhetoric devoted themselves to teaching simply a hollow exercise of using clever tricks, excessively epigrammatic style, extravagant expression, fanciful and fantastic themes, all of which had no vital substance. *Non vitae sed scholae discimus* ("we learn not for life but for school"), said the philosopher Seneca. It is against this corruption of oratory that Quintilian inveighs here and often. In one setting, however, the broad rhetorical education did continue to be reasonably valid, namely in the courts (§§7-8 below). To this Quintilian refers when in §8 below he says: "For if declamation is not a preparation for the actual work of the courts, it can only be compared to the rant of an actor or the raving of a lunatic." Of course, Quintilian did hope that his orator could ultimately be cast in the role of statesman, not merely that of lawyer.

such is the extravagance and ignorance of our declaimers. But it is possible to make a sound use of anything that is naturally sound. The subjects chosen for themes should, therefore, be as true to life as possible, and the actual declamation should, as far as may be, be modelled on the pleadings for which it was devised as a training. For we shall hunt in vain among *sponsions* and *interdicts* for magicians and plagues and oracles and stepmothers more cruel than any in tragedy, and other subjects still more unreal than these.[55] What then? Are we never to permit young men to handle unreal or, to be more accurate, poetic themes that they may run riot and exult in their strength and display their full stature? It were best to prohibit them absolutely. But at any rate the themes, however swelling and magnificent, should not be such as to seem foolish and laughable to the eye of an intelligent observer. Consequently, if we must make some concession, let us allow the declaimer to gorge himself occasionally, as long as he realises that his case will be like that of cattle that have blown themselves out with a surfeit of green food: they are cured of their disorder by blood-letting and then put back to food such as will maintain their strength; similarly the declaimer must be rid of his superfluous fat, and his corrupt humours must be discharged, if he wants to be strong and healthy. Otherwise, the first time he makes any serious effort, his swollen emptiness will stand revealed.

Those, however, who hold that declamation has absolutely nothing in common with pleading in the courts, are clearly quite unaware of the reasons which gave rise to this type of exercise. For if declamation is not a preparation for the actual work of the courts, it can only be compared to the rant of an actor or the raving of a lunatic. For what is the use of attempting to conciliate a non-existent judge, or of stating a case which all know to be false, or of trying to prove a point on which judgment will never be passed? Such waste of effort is, however, a comparative trifle. But what can be more ludicrous than to work oneself into a passion and to attempt to excite the anger or grief of our hearers, unless we are preparing ourselves by such mimic combats for the actual strife and the pitched battles of the law-courts? Is there then no difference between our declamations and genuine forensic ora-

---

55. *Sponsions* and *interdicts* are serious legal terms which represent the kinds of cases to which our orator-lawyer would have to speak in court, whereas the other declamatory topics mentioned here are fanciful, unreal, far removed from life. One can see here and below something about our current byword "relevance."

tory? I can reply, that if we speak with a desire for improvement, there will be no difference. I wish indeed that certain additions could be made to the existing practice; that we made use of names, that our fictitious debates dealt with more complicated cases and sometimes took longer to deliver, that we were less afraid of words drawn from everyday speech and that we were in the habit of seasoning our words with jests. For as regards all these points, we are mere novices when we come to actual pleading, however elaborate the training that the schools have given us on other points.

And even if display is the object of declamation, surely we ought to unbend a little for the entertainment of our audience. For even in those speeches which, although undoubtedly to some extent concerned with the truth, are designed to charm the multitude (such for instance as panegyrics and the oratory of display in all its branches), it is permissible to be more ornate and not merely to disclose all the resources of our art, which in cases of law should as a rule be concealed, but actually to flaunt them before those who have been summoned to hear us. Declamation therefore should resemble the truth, since it is modelled on forensic and deliberative oratory. On the other hand it also involves an element of display, and should in consequence assume a certain air of elegance. In this connexion I may cite the practice of comic actors, whose delivery is not exactly that of common speech, since that would be inartistic, but is on the other hand not far removed from the accents of nature, for, if it were, their mimicry would be a failure: what they do therefore is to exalt the simplicity of ordinary speech by a touch of stage decoration. So too we shall have to put up with certain inconveniences arising from the nature of our fictitious themes; such draw-backs occur more especially in connexion with those numerous details which are left uncertain and which we presume to suit our purpose, such as the ages of our characters, their wealth, their families, or the strength, laws and manners of the cities where our scenes are laid, and the like. Sometimes we even draw arguments from the actual flaws of the assumptions involved by the theme. But each of these points shall be dealt with in its proper place. For although the whole purpose of this work is the formation of an orator, I have no intention of passing over anything that has a genuine connex-

(Higher Education) Bk. II.x, xi

xi.1-7. *Quintilian censures and ridicules the stupid, bombastic rhetors who think that careful instruction in the exacting rules of rhetoric, as advocated by Quintilian, is not necessary. They scorn the discipline of any exacting method, of unity, and of coherence; and they think that it is enough to concoct purple patches and simply string them together. If this sort of thing is all that is necessary, then good-bye to any theory of oratory.*

I have now arrived at the point when I must begin to deal with that portion of the art at which those who have omitted the preceding stages generally commence. I can see, however, that certain critics will attempt to obstruct my path at the very outset; for they will urge that eloquence can dispense with rules of this kind and, in smug satisfaction with themselves and the ordinary methods and exercises of the schools, will laugh at me for my pains; in which they will be only following the example of certain professors of no small reputation. They make it their boast that they speak on impulse and owe their success to their native powers; they further assert that there is no need of proof or careful marshalling of facts when we are speaking on fictitious themes, but only of some of those sounding epigrams, the expectation of which has filled the lecture-room; and these they say are best improvised on the spur of the moment. Further, owing to their contempt for method, when they are meditating on some future effusion, they spend whole days looking at the ceiling in the hope that some magnificent inspiration may occur to them, or rock their bodies to and fro, booming inarticulately as if they had a trumpet inside them and adapting their agitated movements, not to the delivery of the words, but to their pursuit. Some again settle on certain definite openings long before they have thought what they are going to say, with a view to using them as pegs for subsequent snatches of eloquence, and then after practising their delivery first in silent thought and then aloud for hours together, in utter desperation of providing any connecting links, abandon them and take refuge in one formula after another, each no less hackneyed and familiar than the last. The last unreasonable of them devote their attention not to actual cases, but to their purple patches, in the composition of which they pay no attention to the subject-matter, but fire off a series of isolated thoughts just as

ion with the practice of the schools, for fear that students may complain of the omission.

they happen to come to hand. The result is a speech which, being 7
composed of disconnected passages having nothing in common
with each other, must necessarily lack cohesion[56] and can only be
compared to a schoolboy's notebook, in which he jots down any
passages from the declamations of others that have come in for a
word of praise. None the less they do occasionally strike out some
good things and some fine epigrams, such as they make their
boast. Why not? Slaves and barbarians sometimes achieve the
same effects, and if we are to be satisfied with this sort of thing,
then good-bye to any theory of oratory.

*xii.1-12. The claimed merits and the actual defects of the untrained
speaker; the superiority of the trained. Learning removes the defects. A
picture of the performance of the untrained. You may find not merely
forensic pleaders but, what is far more shameful, teachers as well, who
after a brief training in the art of speaking throw method to the wind and
run riot in every direction, abusing those who hold literature in higher
respect and calling them the worst name that occurs to them.*

I must, however, admit that the general opinion is that the 1
untrained speaker is usually the more vigorous. This opinion is
due primarily to the erroneous judgment of faulty critics, who
think that true vigour is all the greater for its lack of art, regarding
it as a special proof of strength to force what might be opened, to
break what might be untied and to drag what might be led. Even a 2
gladiator who plunges into the fight with no skill at arms to help
him, and a wrestler who puts forth the whole strength of his body
the moment he has got a hold, is acclaimed by them for his
outstanding vigour, although it is of frequent occurrence in such
cases for the latter to be overthrown by his own strength and for
the former to find the fury of his onslaught parried by his adver-
sary with a supple turn of the wrist. But there are many details in 3
this department of our art which the unskilled critic will never
notice. For instance, careful division under heads, although
of the utmost importance in actual cases, makes the outward show

---

56. Observe in §§ 1,3,4,6 the phrases and sentences which paint a picture of
irresponsible teachers who have no use for orderly thinking, method, and discipline in composition, with the result that their pupils have developed no sense of
unity and coherence in their writing. Alas, the same sad results are still to be seen
in the work of students who have had the misfortune to pass without adequate
discipline. Discipline is here used in its original sense of teaching, instruction,
thorough training in accordance with rules—which, say what one will, is a sine qua
non of any kind of education.

of strength seem less than the reality; the unhewn block is larger than the polished marble, and things when scattered seem more numerous than when placed together. There is moreover a sort 4 of resemblance between certain merits and certain defects: abuse passes for freedom of speech, rashness for courage, prodigality for abundance. But the untrained advocate will abuse too openly and too often, even though by so doing he imperils the success of the case which he has undertaken and not seldom his own personal safety as well. But even such violence will win men's 5 good opinion, since they are only too pleased to hear another say things which nothing would have induced them to utter themselves. Such speakers are also less careful to avoid that other peril, the pitfall of style, and are so reckless in their efforts that sometimes in their passion for extravagance they light upon some really striking expression. But such success is rare and does not compensate for their other defects.

For the same reason the uninstructed sometimes appear to 6 have a richer flow of language, because they say everything that can be said, while the learned exercise discrimination and self-restraint. To this must be added the fact that such persons take no trouble to prove their contentions, and consequently steer clear of the chilly reception given in our decadent law-courts to arguments and questions and seek only for such themes as may beguile the ears of the public even at the cost of appealing to the most perverted tastes. Again, their epigrams, the sole objects of 7 their quest, seem all the more striking because of the dreariness and squalor of their context, sinced flashes are more clearly seen against a background, not of mere "shade," as Cicero says, but of pitchy darkness. Well, let the world credit them with as much genius as it pleases, so long as it is admitted that such praise is an insult to any man of real eloquence. None the less it must be 8 confessed that learning does take something from oratory, just as the file takes something from rough surfaces or the whetstone from blunt edges or age from wine; it takes away defects, and if the results produced after subjection to the polish of literary study are less, they are less only because they are better.

But these creatures have another weapon in their armoury: 9 they seek to obtain the reputation of speaking with greater vigour than the trained orator by means of their delivery. For they shout on all and every occasion and bellow their every utterance "with uplifted hand," to use their own phrase, dashing this way and that, panting, gesticulating wildly and wagging their heads with all the frenzy of a lunatic. Smite your hands together, stamp the ground, slap your thigh, your breast, your forehead, and you will go straight to the heart of the dingier members of your audience. But the educated speaker, just as he knows how to moderate his style, and to impart variety and artistic form to his speech, is an equal adept in the matter of delivery and will suit his action to the tone of each portion of his utterances, while if he has any one canon for universal observance, it is that he should both possess the reality and present the appearance of self-control. But the ranters confer the title of force on that which is really violence. You may also occasionally find not merely pleaders, but, what is far more shameful, teachers as well, who, after a brief training in the art of speaking, throw method to the winds and, yielding to the impulse of the moment, run riot in every direction, abusing those who hold literature in higher respect as fools without life, courage or vigour, and calling them the first and worst name that occurs to them.[57] Still let me congratulate these gentlemen on attaining eloquence without industry, method or study. As for myself I have long since retired from the task of teaching in the schools and of speaking in the courts, thinking it the most honourable conclusion to retire while my services were still in request, and all I ask is to be allowed to console my leisure by making such researches and composing such instructions as will, I hope, prove useful to young men of ability, and are, at any rate, a pleasure to myself.

xiii.1-8,14-17. Rules: most authors of textbooks have laid down a rigid code of rules such as for the formal parts of an oration. But Quintilian refuses to impose on students of rhetoric a rigid code, a system of laws as immutable as fate. To be sure, rules are generally useful, but an orator should be free to modify them in order to meet varying emergencies. Quintilian does not want young men to think their education complete when they have mastered one of the many small textbooks in circulation. For the art of speaking can only be attained by hard work, unremitting study, a variety of exercises, repeated trial, highest prudence, and unfailing quickness of good judgment.

57. "A little learning is a dangerous thing." Inadequately trained speakers, teachers, et al., are sometimes stupid enough to think that they know it all; and they can be overbearing even to those of greater experience and knowledge, thus giving themselves away. Contrast the self-control of the educated speaker just above.

(Higher Education) Bk. II.xii, xiii

Let no one however demand from me a rigid code of rules such as most authors of textbooks have laid down, or ask me to impose on students of rhetoric a system of laws immutable as fate, a system in which injunctions as to the *exordium*[58] and its nature lead the way; then come the *statement of facts* and the laws to be observed in this connexion: next the *proposition* or, as some prefer, the *digression,* followed by prescriptions as to the order in which the various questions should be discussed, with all the other rules, which some speakers follow as though they had no choice, but to regard them as orders and as if it were a crime to take any other line. If the whole of rhetoric could be thus embodied in one compact code, it would be an easy task of little compass: but most rules are liable to be altered by the nature of the case, circumstances of time and place, and by hard necessity itself. Consequently the all-important gift for an orator is a wise adaptability since he is called upon to meet the most varied emergencies. What if you should instruct a general, as often as he marshals his troops for battle, to draw up his front in line, advance his wings to left and right, and station his cavalry to protect his flank? This will perhaps be the best plan, if circumstances allow. But it may have to be modified owing to the nature of the ground, if, for instance, he is confronted by a mountain, if a river bars his advance, or his movements are hampered by hills, woods or broken country. Or again it may be modified by the character of the enemy or the nature of the crisis by which he is faced. On one occasion he will fight in line, on another in column, on one he will use his auxiliary troops, on another his legionaries; while occasionally a feint of flight may win the day. So, too, with the rules of oratory. Is the *exordium* necessary or superfluous? should it be long or short? addressed entirely to the judge or sometimes directed to some other quarter by the employment of some figure of speech? Should the statement of facts be concise or developed at some length? continuous or divided into sections? and should it follow the actual or an artificial order of events? The orator will find the answers to all these questions in the circumstances of the case. So, too, with the order in which questions should be discussed, since in any given debate it may often suit one party best that such and such a question come up first, while their opponents would be best suited by another. For these rules have not the formal authority of laws or decrees of the plebs, but are, with all they

1

2

3

4

5

6

58. See note 36 above.

contain, the children of expediency. I will not deny that it is generally expedient to conform to such rules, otherwise I should not be writing now; but if our friend expediency suggests some other course to us, why, we shall disregard the authority of the professors and follow her.

For my part above all things
   "This I enjoin and urge and urge anew"[59]
that in all his pleadings the orator should keep two things constantly in view, what is becoming[60] and what is expedient. But it is often expedient and occasionally becoming to make some modification in the time-honoured order. It has always, therefore, been my custom not to tie myself down to *universal* or *general* rules (this being the nearest equivalent I can find for the Greek *catholic rules*). For rules are rarely of such a kind that their validity cannot be shaken and overthrown in some particular or other.

But I must reserve each of these points for fuller treatment in its proper place. For the present I will only say that I do not want young men to think their education complete when they have mastered one of the small text-books of which so many are in circulation, or to ascribe a talismanic value to the arbitrary decrees of theorists. The art of speaking can only be attained by hard work and assiduity of study, by a variety of exercises and repeated trial, the highest prudence and unfailing quickness of judgment.[61] But rules are helpful all the same so long as they indicate the direct road and do not restrict us absolutely to the ruts made by others. For he who thinks it an unpardonable sin to leave the old, old track, must be content to move at much the same speed as a tight-rope walker. Thus, for example, we often leave a paved military road to take a short cut or, finding that the direct route is impossible owing to floods having broken down the bridges, are forced to make a circuit, while if our house is on fire and flames bar the way to the front door, we make our escape by breaking through a party wall. The orator's task covers a large ground, is extremely varied and develops some new aspect almost every day, so that the last word on the subject will never have been said. I shall however try to set forth the traditional rules and to point out their best features, mentioning the changes, additions and subtractions which seem desirable.

59. Virgil, *Aeneid*, III.436.
60. I.e., proper, fitting.
61. All this can be said equally well about the art of teaching, with special emphasis on hard work, Quintilian's recurrent gospel of labor.

(Higher Education) Bk. II.xiii, xvi

xvi.1-6. Is rhetoric, i.e. eloquence, useful? Some denounce eloquence because of its potential for harm. Quintilian cites examples of this.

There follows the question as to whether rhetoric is useful. 1
Some are in the habit of denouncing it most violently and of shamelessly employing the powers of oratory to accuse oratory itself. "It is eloquence" they say "that snatches criminals from the 2 penalties of the law, eloquence that from time to time secures the condemnation of the innocent and leads deliberation astray, eloquence that stirs up not merely sedition and popular tumult, but wars beyond all expiation, and that is most effective when it makes falsehood prevail over truth." The comic poets even accuse 3 Socrates of teaching how to make the worse cause seem the better,[62] while Plato says that Gorgias and Tisias made similar

62. The Greek comic poet Aristophanes in his play the *Clouds* (423 B.C.) devastatingly satirized the new trends in education at Athens in the latter part of the fifth century B.C. In a *direct* democracy such as Athens the ability to speak effectively in public became increasingly important: (A) in politics where the ordinary citizen could not only run for at least some offices but could introduce to the assembly a bill (which he would have to support by whatever oratorical ability he possessed) and could debate public policy; (B) in the law courts, where a citizen had to plead his own case in person; (C) before the people on public occasions of various sorts. Though oratory had existed from Homer's time on, there now arose to meet this increasing need for oratorical prowess in the fifth century a group of men called Sophists (originally meaning "wise men"), who said that they could teach the art of effective and persuasive speech and gave lectures or courses by which to achieve this goal and for which they charged tuition fees. The Sophists, then, were professors of rhetoric and higher education. Since the demand was primarily that they teach how to speak persuasively, most of them were not greatly concerned about morality; and in time they acquired the reputation of teaching by sophistic quibbles how to prove any point, whether right or wrong, and even in the last analysis how to prove that the wrong was right and the right was wrong or, in other words, "to make the worse cause seem the better." Hence the connotation of our word "sophistry" today. In the *Clouds* Aristophanes, unjustly but for humorous and satirical effect, casts the famous, eccentric philosopher Socrates as the protagonist of all that was evil in the Sophists and their new education. Then in the famous debate between the Right Logos (the old method of education) and the Wrong Logos (the new method of education), Aristophanes sets forth the virtues inculcated by the older education (e.g., justice, truth, reason, virtue, modesty, morality, respect for elders, good physical exercise and physique, endurance of hardship for country and honor, the heroes of Marathon); and he then shows how the new education of the Sophists (the Wrong Logos) rejects all the values and virtues of the old education, is a corrupter of youth, is opposed to physical exercise but favors indulgence, intemperance, immorality, confutes the laws, uses rationalism against the old religion, and is generally guilty of sophistry. In the end the Right Logos admits that he has been beaten because the majority of the Athenians are now in favor of the Wrong Logos and are stronger!

professions. And to these they add further examples drawn from the history of Rome and Greece, enumerating all those who used their pernicious eloquence not merely against individuals but against whole states and threw an ordered commonwealth into a state of turmoil or even brought it to utter ruin; and they point out that for this very reason rhetoric was banished from Sparta, while its powers were cut down at Athens itself by the fact that an orator was forbidden to stir the passions of his audience. On the showing of these critics not only orators but generals, magistrates, medicine and philosophy itself will all be useless. Doctors have been caught using poisons, and those who falsely assume the name of philosopher have occasionally been detected in the gravest crimes. Let us give up eating, it often makes us ill; let us never go inside houses, for sometimes they collapse on their occupants; let never a sword be forged for a soldier, since it might be used by a robber. And who does not realise that fire and water, both necessities of life, and, to leave mere earthly things, even the sun and moon, the greatest of the heavenly bodies, are occasionally capable of doing harm.

xvi.7-10. Then follow powerful examples of instances where the orator by his eloquence has greatly benefited the state and his fellowmen. Therefore, although eloquence can be used for good or ill, it is unfair to regard as evil that which can be employed for good.

On the other hand will it be denied that it was by his gift of speech that Appius the Blind broke off the dishonourable peace which was on the point of being concluded with Pyrrhus?[63] Did not the divine eloquence of Cicero win popular applause even when he denounced tha Agrarian laws,[64] did it not crush the audacious plots of Catiline[65] and win, while he still wore the garb of civil life, the highest honour that can be conferred on a victorious general, a public thanksgiving to heaven? Has not oratory often revived the courage of a panic-stricken army and per-

63. In 280 B.C. Appius Claudius the famous censor, though now blind and aged, by his oratory persuaded the Roman Senate to reject the peace proposals of the Greek general Pyrrhus.

64. The Agrarian laws of 64 B.C. were calculated to be popular and were drawn up primarily to increase the power of Julius Caesar; but Cicero's oratory defeated them.

65. In 63 B.C. Cicero's famous orations against Catiline thwarted the Catilinarian conspiracy to take over the government at Rome and to rule for their own aggrandizement.

(Higher Education) Bk. II.xvi

suaded the soldier faced by all the perils of war that glory is a fairer thing than life itself? Nor shall the history of Sparta and Athens move me more than that of the Roman people, who have always held the orator in highest honour. Never in my opinion would the founders of cities have induced their unsettled multitudes to form communities had they not moved them by the magic of their eloquence: never without the highest gifts of oratory would the great legislators have constrained mankind to submit themselves to the yoke of law. Nay, even the principles which should guide our life, however fair they may be by nature, yet have greater power to mould the mind to virtue, when the beauty of things is illumined by the splendour of eloquence. Wherefore, although the weapons of oratory may be used either for good or ill, it is unfair to regard that as an evil which can be employed for good.

xvi.11-19. God gave to other animals many gifts which man does not possess; but he gave to man the special gifts of speech and reason. However, the power of reason cannot be very helpful without the ability to express our thoughts in speech. Therefore, since the art of effective speaking is of such tremendous value for ourselves and our fellowmen, should we not strive to cultivate the greatest possible excellence in the use of speech?

These problems, however, may be left to those who hold that rhetoric is the power to persuade. If our definition of rhetoric as the science of speaking well implies that an orator must be a good man, there can be no doubt about its usefulness. And in truth that god, who was in the beginning, the father of all things and the architect of the universe, distinguished man from all other living creatures that are subject to death, by nothing more than this, that he gave him the gift of speech. For as regards physical bulk, strength, robustness, endurance or speed, man is surpassed in certain cases by dumb beasts, who also are far more independent of external assistance. They know by instinct without need of any teacher how to move rapidly, to feed themselves and swim. Many too have their bodies clothed against cold, possess natural weapons and have not to search for their food, whereas in all these respects man's life is full of toil. Reason then was the greatest gift of the Almighty, who willed that we should share its possession with the immortal gods. But reason by itself would help us but little and would be far less evident in us, had we not the power to express our thoughts in speech;[66] for it is the lack of this power rather than thought and understanding, which they do to a certain extent possess, that is the great defect in other living things. The construction of a soft lair, the weaving of nests, the hatching and rearing of their young, and even the storing up of food for the coming winter, together with certain other achievements which we cannot imitate, such as the making of honey and wax, all these perhaps indicate the possession of a certain degree of reason; but since the creatures that do these things lack the gift of speech they are called dumb and unreasoning beasts. Finally, how little the heavenly boon of reason avails those who are born dumb. If therefore we have received no fairer gift from heaven than speech, what shall we regard as so worthy of laborious cultivation, or in what should we sooner desire to excel our fellow-men, than that in which mankind excels all other living things? And we should be all the more eager to do so, since there is no art which yields a more grateful recompense for the labour bestowed upon it. This will be abundantly clear if we consider the origins of oratory and the progress it has made; and it is capable of advancing still further. I will not stop to point out how useful and how becoming a task it is for a good man to defend his friends, to guide the senate by his counsels, and to lead peoples or armies to follow his bidding; I merely ask, is it not a noble thing, by employing the understanding which is common to mankind and the words that are used by all, to win such honour and glory that you seem not to speak or plead, but rather, as was said of Pericles, to thunder and lighten?

xix.1-3. Nature and art: does nature or education contribute more to eloquence? Nature can accomplish much without the aid of education but education can accomplish nothing without nature. The best results occur when both nature and education are blended together.

I quite realise that there is a further question as to whether eloquence derives most from nature or from education. This

---

66. One could write an essay on the topic that however great our powers of reason and however great and beneficial our ideas, all this reasoning and these ideas will accomplish very little if we cannot communicate them to our fellow men clearly and persuasively. Consequently, since language is one of our most valuable tools, *every* student should have thorough, unremitting discipline (training) and exercises in accurate and effective language written and oral throughout his entire schooling. The study of language is not merely for oratory; it is for everyday use in every field.

(Higher Education) Bk. II.xvi, xix, xxi

question really lies outside the scope of our inquiry, since the ideal orator must necessarily be the result of a blend of both. But I do regard it as of great importance that we should decide how far there is any real question on this point. For if we make an absolute divorce between the two, nature will still be able to accomplish much without the aid of education, while the latter is valueless without the aid of nature. If, on the other hand, they are blended in equal proportions, I think we shall find that the average orator owes most to nature, while the perfect orator owes more to education. We may take a parallel from agriculture. A thoroughly barren soil will not be improved even by the best cultivation, while good land will yield some useful produce without cultivation; but in the case of really rich land cultivation will do more for it than its own natural fertility. To conclude, nature is the raw material for education: the one forms, the other is formed. Without material art can do nothing, material without art does possess a certain value, while the perfection of art is better than the best material.

xxi.4-6,14-20,22-23. The subject matter of oratory is everything that may be placed before it as a subject for speech. Thus, while an orator can hardly be expected to start out with a total knowledge of everything, yet through study of things not previously studied or experienced, he should be able to speak on anything—construction work, architectural matters, music, medicine, measurements, and what not; and he will naturally by his training be able to present the pertinent matters (outside of the strictly technical points) more effectively than can the artist, scientist, craftsman, or ordinary person who has not had his education.

For my own part, and I have authority to support me, I hold that the material of rhetoric is composed of everything that may be placed before it as a subject for speech. Plato, if I read him aright, makes Socrates[67] say to Gorgias that its material is to be found in things not words. Cicero[68] expresses his opinion that the orator has to speak about all kinds of things; I will quote his actual words: "although the very meaning of the name of orator and the fact that he professes to speak well seem to imply a promise and undertaking that the orator will speak with elegance and fullness on any subject that may be put before him." And in another passage he says, "It is the duty of the true orator to seek out, hear, read, discuss, handle and ponder everything that befalls in the

67. Plato, *Gorgias*, 449 E.
68. Cicero, *de Oratore*, I.vi.21.

life of man, since it is with this that the orator is concerned and this that forms the material with which he has to deal."[69]

There is a further objection made by certain critics, who say "Well then, if an orator has to speak on every subject, he must be the master of all the arts." I might answer this criticism in the words of Cicero,[70] in whom I find the following passage:—"In my opinion no one can be an absolutely perfect orator unless he has acquired a knowledge of all important subjects and arts." I however regard it as sufficient that an orator should not be actually ignorant of the subject on which he has to speak. For he cannot have a knowledge of all causes, and yet he should be able to speak on all. On what then will he speak? On those which he has studied. Similarly as regards the arts, he will study those concerning which he has to speak, as occasion may demand, and will speak on those which he has studied.

What then?—I am asked—will not a builder speak better on the subject of building and a musician on music? Certainly, if the orator does not know what is the question at issue. Even an illiterate peasant who is a party to a suit will speak better on behalf of his case than an orator who does not know what the subject in dispute may be. But on the other hand if the orator receive instruction from the builder or the musician, he will put forward what he has thus learned better than either, just as he will plead a case better than his client, once he has been instructed in it. The builder and the musician will, however, speak on the subject of their respective arts, if there should be any technical point which requires to be established. Neither will be an orator, but he will perform his task like an orator, just as when an untrained person binds up a wound, he will not be a physician, but he will be acting as one. Is it suggested that such topics never crop up in panegyric, deliberative or forensic oratory? When the question of the construction of a port at Ostia came up for discussion, had not the orator to state his views? And yet it was a subject requiring the technical knowledge of the architect. Does not the orator discuss the question whether livid spots and swellings on the body are symptomatic of ill-health or poison? And yet that is a question for the qualified physician. Will he not deal with

69. Ibid., III.xiv.54. Similarly it is valuable for a teacher to have the widest acquaintance with all kinds of such things vicariously if not actually. For thus he can relate to a wider range of people and subjects.
70. Ibid., I.vi.20.

measurements and figures? And yet we must admit that they form part of mathematics. For my part I hold that practically all subjects are under certain circumstances liable to come up for treatment by the orator. If the circumstances do not occur, the subjects will not concern him.

We were therefore right in asserting that the material of rhetoric is composed of everything that comes before the orator for treatment, an assertion which is confirmed by the practice of everyday speech. For there is nothing which may not crop up in a cause or appear as a question for discussion. Aristotle himself also by his tripartite division of oratory, into forensic, deliberative and demonstrative, practically brought everything into the orator's domain, since there is nothing that may not come up for treatment by one of these three kinds of rhetoric.

BOOK III

EXCERPTS FROM CHAPTER I

(Origin and Types of Oratory)

III.i.1-5. In Book III Quintilian proposes to discuss the origin, parts, and methods of the art of rhetoric, or oratory; but he is worried that the necessary exposition of rules may turn the students off.

I shall now discuss its [referring to the art of rhetoric, or oratory] origin, its component parts, and the method to be adopted in handling and forming our conception of each. For most authors of text-books have stopped short of this, indeed Apollodorus confines himself solely to forensic oratory. I know that those who asked me to write this work were specially interested in that portion on which I am now entering, and which, owing to the necessity of examining a great diversity of opinions, at once forms by far the most difficult section of this work, and also, I fear, may be the least attractive to my readers, since it necessitates a dry exposition of rules. In other portions of this work I have attempted to introduce a certain amount of ornateness, not, I may say, to advertise my style (if I had wished to do that, I could have chosen a more fertile theme), but in order that I might thus do something to lure our young men to make themselves acquainted with those principles which I regarded as necessary to the study of rhetoric: for I hoped that by giving them something which was not unpleasant to read I might induce a greater readiness to learn those rules which I feared might, by the

(Origin and Types of Oratory) Bk. III.i

dryness and aridity which must necessarily characterise their exposition, revolt their minds[1] and offend their ears which are nowadays grown somewhat over-sensitive. Lucretius has the same object in mind when he states that he has set forth his philosophical system in verse; for you will remember the well-known simile which he uses:—

"And as physicians when they seek to give
A draught of bitter wormwood to a child,
First smear along the edge that rims the cup
The liquid sweets of honey, golden-hued,"

and the rest.[2] But I fear that this book will have too little honey and too much wormwood, and that though the student may find it a healthy draught, it will be far from agreeable.

III.i.5-7. The infinite diversity of opinion and disputes among authors, who, though aiming at the same goal, follow diverse paths to that goal and who "have altered even that which was perfectly sound in order to establish a claim to originality."

I am also haunted by the further fear that it will be all the less attractive from the fact that most of the precepts which it contains are not original, but derived from others,[3] and because it is likely to rouse the opposition of certain persons who do not share my views. For there are a large number of writers, who though they are all moving toward the same goal, have constructed different roads to it and each drawn their followers into their own. The latter, however, approve of the path on which they have been launched whatever its nature, and it is difficult to change the convictions implanted in boyhood, for the excellent reason that

1. Again we read Quintilian's earnest concern that textbooks should preferably not be dry but should be as interesting and attractive as possible. It is also instructive to observe that the ancient Roman students were as likely to be turned off by "a dry exposition of rules" as are our modern students (see Book I.Pref.24 and note). The clear lesson for teachers is that they must *exert themselves* to present their subjects as attractively and humanely as possible; and the lesson for students is that in school and in life not all the necessary things can be equally interesting, but they have to be confronted and endured for the sake of "a sound mind in a sound body."

2. Lucretius, *On the Nature of Things*, I.936-38 and ff. and IV.11-13 and ff., where Lucretius in much the same fashion seeks to render agreeable his somewhat bitter, forbidding philosophy of atomic materialism in which there was no real place for the gods of old. Cp. also Horace, *Satires*, I.I.25-26: "as coaxing teachers at times give cookies to children so that they may be willing to learn their ABC's."

3. Note Quintilian's refreshing modesty and honesty in not making any special claims of originality here. Cp. note 4 and §22 below.

everybody prefers to have learned rather than to be in process of learning. But, as will appear in the course of this book, there is an infinite diversity of opinions among writers on this subject, since some have added their own discoveries to those portions of the art which were still shapeless and unformed, and subsequently have altered even what was perfectly sound in order to establish a claim to originality.[4]

III.i.22. Quintilian intends to be independent in expressing his own opinions; but he conscientiously cites the opinions of many other authors, and readers are to be left free to choose as they please.

Still, although so many writers have preceded me, I shall not shrink from expressing my own opinion on certain points. I am not a superstitious adherent of any school, and as this book will contain a collection of the opinions of many different authors, it was desirable to leave it to my readers to select what they will. I shall be content if they praise me for my industry, wherever there is no scope for originality.

---

4. Perhaps it should not be surprising that the pedagogical passion to earn a reputation for originality goes back two thousand years and is still burning today, if one can judge from the many educational innovations of recent date. In part this can be perfectly natural and legitimate, i.e., when something really needs to be changed for the better. However, when an educationist seeks to alter needlessly that which was already perfectly sound, he opens himself to the suspicion of advocating a new fad primarily for the sake of a reputation for originality. In this there is little virtue but much vanity. What a pity that so much time and expense and human effort have to be spent to sift out the sound kernels of necessary reform from the chaff of ephemeral fad!

BOOK IV

EXCERPTS FROM CHAPTER II

(Excellence in Communication of Facts)

IV.ii.31,33. Three stylistic virtues to be observed in composing the part of a speech known as the narratio *(narrative, or statement of facts): (1) lucidity (clearness), (2) brevity, (3) plausibility (credibility). These qualities will enable the judge more easily to understand, remember, and believe what we say.*

I will now proceed to the method to be adopted in making our statement of facts. The *statement of facts* consists in the persuasive exposition of that which either has been done, or is supposed to have been done, or, to quote the definition given by Apollodorus, is a speech instructing the audience as to the nature of the case in dispute. Most writers, more especially those of the Isocratean school, hold that it should be lucid, brief and plausible (for it is of no importance if we substitute clear for lucid, or credible or probable for plausible). The *statement* will be either wholly in our favour or wholly in that of our opponent or a mixture of both. If it is entirely in our own favour, we may rest content with the three qualities just mentioned, the result of which is to make it easier for the judge to understand, remember and believe what we say.

IV.ii.34-35. Plausibility.

Now I should regret that anyone should censure my conduct in suggesting that a *statement* which is wholly in our favour should be *plausible,* when as a matter of fact it is *true.* There are many things which are true, but scarcely credible, just as there are many things which are plausible though false. It will therefore require just as much exertion on our part to make the judge believe what we say when it is true as it will when it is fictitious. These good qualities, which I have mentioned above, do not indeed cease to be virtues in other portions of the speech; for it is our duty to avoid obscurity in every part of our pleading.

IV.ii.36-37,39. Lucidity, or clearness, is essential for ease of comprehension; but the ostentatious and extravagant language of so many speakers makes the case unintelligible.

We shall achieve lucidity and clearness[1] in our statement of facts, first by setting forth our story in words which are appropriate, significant and free from any taint of meanness, but not on the other hand farfetched or unusual, and secondly by giving a distinct account of facts, persons, times, places and causes, while our delivery must be adapted to our matter, so that the judge will take in what we say with the utmost readiness. This latter virtue is disregarded by the majority of speakers who are used to the noisy applause of a large audience. When such persons as these get a fair field for stating their case, they select this as the precise occasion for affected modulations of the voice, throwing back their heads, thumping their sides and indulging in every kind of extravagance of statement, language and style. As a result, while the speech, from its very monstrosity, meets with applause, the case remains unintelligible. However, let us pass to another subject; my aim is to win favour for pointing out the right road rather than to give offence by rebuking such perversity.

IV.ii.40-47. Brevity, or the virtue of multum in parvo: *avoid irrelevance; include nothing more than the case demands. Examples cited. Repetitions, tautologies, and diffuseness must be avoided just as must any obscurity resulting from excessive brevity. Cultivate the happy mean in language.*

The *statement of facts* will be brief, if in the first place we start at that point of the case at which it begins to concern the judge, secondly avoid irrelevance, and finally cut out everything the removal of which neither hampers the activities of the judge nor harms our own case. For frequently conciseness of detail is not inconsistent with length in the whole. Take for instance such a

1. For other statements about the cardinal importance of clearness in our communications see II.iii.8 and note 18 thereon; VIII.ii.22-23.

statement as the following: "I came to the harbour, I saw a ship, I asked the cost of a passage, the price was agreed, I went on board, the anchor was weighed, we loosed our cable and set out." Nothing could be terser than these assertions, but it would have been quite sufficient to say "I sailed from the harbour." And whenever the conclusion gives a sufficiently clear idea of the premises, we must be content with having given a hint which will enable our audience to understand what we have left unsaid. Consequently when it is possible to say "I have a young son," it is quite superfluous to say, "Being desirous of children I took a wife, a son was born whom I acknowledged and reared and brought up to manhood." For this reason some of the Greeks draw a distinction between a concise statement and a brief statement, the former being free from all superfluous matter, while the latter may conceivably omit something that requires to be stated. Personally, when I use the word brevity, I mean not saying less, but not saying more than occasion demands. As for repetitions and tautologies and diffuseness, which some writers of textbooks tell us we must avoid, I pass them by; they are faults which we should shun for other reasons beside our desire for brevity. But we must be equally on our guard against the obscurity which results from excessive abridgment, and it is better to say a little more than is necessary than a little less. For though a diffuse irrelevance is tedious, the omission of what is necessary is positively dangerous. ous.

Consequently, we must aim, perhaps everywhere, but above all in our *statement of facts,* at striking the happy mean in our language, and the happy mean may be defined as saying just what is necessary and just what is sufficient. By "just what is necessary" I mean not the bare minimum necessary to convey our meaning; for our brevity must not be devoid of elegance, without which it would be merely uncouth: pleasure beguiles the attention, and that which delights us ever seems less long, just as a picturesque and easy journey tires us less for all its length than a difficult short cut through an arid waste. And I would never carry my desire for brevity so far as to refuse admission to details which may contribute to the plausibility of our narrative.

BOOK VIII

EXCERPTS FROM PREFACE AND CHAPTER II

(Vocabulary Enrichment and Clearness in Style)

VIII. Preface 28-29. The orator needs a copious supply of words acquired by wide reading and strengthened by continual exercise.

On the other hand, if he (the orator) will only first form a true conception of the principles of eloquence, accumulate a copious supply of words[1] by wide and suitable reading, apply the art of arrangement to the words thus acquired, and finally, by continual exercise, develop strength to use his acquisitions so that every word is ready at hand and lies under his very eyes, he will never lose a single word. For the man who follows these instructions will find that facts and words appropriate to their expression will present themselves spontaneously. But it must be remembered that a long course of preliminary study is necessary and that the requisite ability must not merely be acquired, but carefully stored for use.

ii.17-19,22-23. But Quintilian condemns verbosity, obscurity, and extreme brevity. For clearness is the first essential of good style.

Again, some writers introduce a whole host of useless words;

---

1. The prime importance of a copious vocabulary is with good reason frequently emphasized by Quintilian. See, for instance, II.vii.4, and especially X.i.5-10. It should be no less stressed by us today as invaluable in communications. Every teacher of every subject has the bounden duty to increase constantly and accurately his own vocabulary and that of all his students, for this will prove a lifelong treasure and source of power in the important matter of communications.

for, in their eagerness to avoid ordinary methods of expression, and allured by false ideals of beauty they wrap up everything in a multitude of words simply and solely because they are unwilling to make a direct and simple statement of the facts: and then they link up and involve one of those long-winded clauses with others like it, and extend their periods to a length beyond the compass of mortal breath. Some even expend an infinity of toil to acquire this vice, which, by the way, is nothing new: for I learn from the pages of Livy that there was one, a teacher, who instructed his pupils to make all they said obscure. Others are consumed with a passion for brevity and omit words which are actually necessary to the sense, regarding it as a matter of complete indifference whether their meaning is intelligible to others, so long as they know what they mean themselves. For my own part, I regard as useless words which make such a demand upon the ingenuity of the hearer.

For my own part, I regard clearness[2] as the first essential of a good style; there must be propriety in our words, their order must be straightforward, the conclusion of the period must not be long postponed, there must be nothing lacking and nothing superfluous. Thus our language will be approved by the learned and clear to the uneducated. I am speaking solely of clearness in style, as I have already dealt with clearness in the presentation of facts in the rules I laid down for the *statement of the case*. But the general method is the same in both. For if what we say is not less nor more than is required, and is clear and systematically arranged, the whole matter will be plain and obvious even to a not too attentive audience.

---

2. Another ringing and demanding statement about clearness. Let us heed it! Re clearness in the *narratio* (statement of the case) see IV.ii.36-39 and note 1 thereon.

BOOK X

EXCERPTS FROM CHAPTERS I, III, IV, VII

(Reading and Writing)

Chapter i: The value of reading.

X.i.1-3. In addition to the formal rules of style already discussed there are three essentials for developing oratorical force and power: (1) writing (frequent practice), (2) reading (for models), (3) speaking (oral performance); and they are closely interrelated.

But these rules of style, while part of the student's theoretical knowledge, are not in themselves sufficient to give him oratorical power. In addition he will require that assured facility which the Greeks call *hexis*.[1] I know that many have raised the question as to whether this is best acquired by writing, reading or speaking, and it would indeed be a question calling for serious consideration, if we could rest content with any one of the three. But they are so intimately and inseparably connected, that if one of them be neglected, we shall but waste the labour which we have devoted to the others. For eloquence will never attain to its full development or robust health, unless it acquires strength by frequent practice in writing, while such practice without the models supplied by reading will be like a ship drifting aimlessly without a steersman. Again, he who knows what he ought to say and how he should say it, will be like a miser brooding over his hoarded treasure, unless he has the weapons of his eloquence ready for battle and

---

1. "Possession; a habit" of mind or body.

(Reading and Writing) Bk. X.i

prepared to deal with every emergency. But the degree in which a thing is essential does not necessarily make it of immediate and supreme importance for the formation of the ideal orator. For obviously the power of speech is the first essential, since therein lies the primary task of the orator, and it is obvious that it was with this that the art of oratory began, and that the power of imitation[2] comes next, and third and last diligent practice in writing.

X.i.5-8,10. The importance of a copious vocabulary and how to acquire it.

There can then be no doubt that he must accumulate a certain store of resources, to be employed whenever they may be required. The resources of which I speak consist in a copious supply of words[3] and matter. But while the matter is necessarily either peculiar to the individual case, or at best common to only a few, words must be acquired to suit all and every case. Now, if there were special words adapted to each individual thing, they would require less care, since they would automatically be suggested by the matter in hand. But since some words are more literal, more ornate, more significant or euphonious than others, our orator must not merely be acquainted with all of them, but must have them at his fingers' ends and before his very eyes, so that when they present themselves for his critical selection, he will find it easy to make the appropriate choice. I know that some speakers make a practice of learning lists of synonyms by heart, in order that one word out of the several available may at once present itself to them, and that if, after using one word, they find that it is wanted again after a brief interval, they may be able to select another word with the same meaning and so avoid the necessity of

---

2. In I.iii.1 Quintilian refers to the power of imitation as a sign of a child's educability. In the present section he directs the power of imitation to the models to be imitated as found in the reading of literature, which provides us with a sort of rudder for writing and speaking. Similarly today the judicious and analytical reading of good literature and writings should be a basic subject throughout our modern curricula.

3. Throughout §§ 5-10 here Quintilian again stresses the tremendous importance of a copious vocabulary, which is just as necessary for educated and influential people today as it was in Quintilian's time. See also VIII.Pref.28 and note I thereon; X.vii.7. For us moderns one of the best ways to enlarge and sharpen our knowledge and command of words is to study at least a little Latin. (In fact, where it is taught humanely, students find Latin enjoyable for its own sake and profitable for the understanding and improvement of their own language, critics to the contrary notwithstanding.)

repetition. But this practice is childish and involves thankless labour, while it is really of very little use, as it merely results in the assembly of a disorderly crowd of words, for the speaker to snatch the first that comes to hand.

On the contrary, discrimination[4] is necessary in the acquisition of our stock of words; for we are aiming at true oratory, not at the fluency of a cheapjack. And we shall attain our aim by reading and listening to the best writers and orators, since we shall thus learn not merely the words by which things are to be called, but when each particular word is most appropriate. Now to acquire a knowledge of these words and to be acquainted not merely with their meaning, but with their forms and rhythmical values, so that they may seem appropriate wherever employed, we shall need to read and listen diligently, since all language is received first through the ear.

X.i.16-19. A comparison of the advantages of listening (i.e., to oratory, which is more rapid and emotional) and reading, which is more leisurely, reflective, and critical.

But the advantages conferred by reading and listening are not identical. The speaker stimulates us by the animation of his delivery, and kindles the imagination, not by presenting us with an elaborate picture, but by bringing us into actual touch with the things themselves. Then all is life and movement, and we receive the new-born offspring of his imagination with enthusiastic approval. We are moved not merely by the actual issue of the trial, but by all that the orator himself has at stake. Moreover his voice, the grace of his gestures, the adaptation of his delivery (which is of supreme importance in oratory), and, in a word, all his excellences in combination, have their educative effect. In reading, on the other hand, the critical faculty is a surer guide, inasmuch as the listener's judgment is often swept away by his preference for a particular speaker, or by the applause of an enthusiastic audience. For we are ashamed to disagree with them, and an unconscious modesty prevents us from ranking our own opinion above

---

4. However, simply a large stock of words is not enough; and one must also be able to use these words with discrimination, judgment, and accuracy—an ability which is too seldom cultivated in our own times, for many even among those who ought to know better are too careless or too lazy or both. Above all, let the teacher take especial care! In addition to Quintilian's suggestions a study of etymologies can be for us a great aid to accuracy and the appreciation of nuances.

theirs, though all the time the taste of the majority is vicious, and the *claque* may praise even what does not really deserve approval.[5] On the other hand, it will sometimes also happen that an audience whose taste is bad will fail to award the praise which is due to the most admirable utterances. Reading, however, is free, and does not hurry past us with the speed of oral delivery; we can re-read a passage again and again if we are in doubt about it or wish to fix it in the memory. We must return to what we have read and reconsider it with care, while, just as we do not swallow our food till we have chewed it and reduced it almost to a state of liquefaction to assist the process of digestion, so what we read must not be committed to the memory for subsequent imitation while it is still in a crude state, but must be softened and, if I may use the phrase, reduced to a pulp by frequent re-perusal.

X.i.20,24-26. *Read the best, read it thoroughly, and reread it; but be discriminating and critical. Read speeches.*

For a long time also we should read none save the best authors and such as are least likely to betray our trust in them, while our reading must be almost as thorough as if we were actually transcribing what we read. Nor must we study it merely in parts, but must read through the whole work from cover to cover and then read it afresh, a precept which applies more especially to speeches, whose merits are often deliberately disguised.

The reader must not, however, jump to the conclusion that all that was uttered by the best authors is necessarily perfect.[6] At times they lapse and stagger beneath the weight of their task, indulge their bent or relax their efforts. Sometimes, again, they give the impression of weariness: for example, Cicero thinks that Demosthenes sometimes nods, and Horace says the same of

5. Now, as then, it almost seems as if everybody must be praised indiscriminately; we lack the stamina to declare for excellence from fear of being branded as undemocratic and snobbish. Must excellence always be downgraded to the level of the ordinary, or the lowest common denominator be elevated to the status of excellence? Rather let there be fair and decent recognition of the integrity of both the A's and the C's without any attendant stigma when these are honestly earned both in school and in life. Of course, egotism and conceit in any connection are intolerable.

6. Quintilian makes a good and sane point for all who would read with real discrimination. Not infrequently teachers have tended to put great authors high on a pedestal for undiscriminating worship. If mighty Homer nods, why should not the others occasionally? Actually students become more interested in famous writers if they can feel free to criticize them reasonably.

Homer himself. For despite their greatness they are still but mortal men, and it will sometimes happen that their reader assumes that anything which he finds in them may be taken as a canon of style, with the result that he imitates their defects (and it is always easier to do this than to imitate their excellences) and thinks himself a perfect replica if he succeeds in copying the blemishes of great men. But modesty and circumspection are required in pronouncing judgment on such great men, since there is always the risk of falling into the common fault of condemning what one does not understand. And, if it is necessary to err on one side or the other, I should prefer that the reader should approve of everything than that he should disapprove of much.

X.i.27-28. Read poetry.

Theophrastus says that the reading of poets is of great service to the orator, and has rightly been followed in this view by many. For the poets will give us inspiration as regards the matter, sublimity of language, the power to excite every kind of emotion, and the appropriate treatment of character, while minds that have become jaded owing to the daily wear and tear of the courts will find refreshment in such agreeable study. Consequently Cicero recommends the relaxation provided by the reading of poetry. We should, however, remember that the orator must not follow the poets in everything, more especially in their freedom of language and their license in the use of figures. Poetry has been compared to the oratory of display, and further, aims solely at giving pleasure, which it seeks to secure by inventing what is not merely untrue, but sometimes even incredible.

X.i.31,34. Read history.

History, also, may provide the orator with a nutriment which we may compare to some rich and pleasant juice. But when we read it, we must remember that many of the excellences of the historian require to be shunned by the orator. For history has a certain affinity to poetry and may be regarded as a kind of prose poem,[7] while it is written for the purpose of narrative, not of proof, and designed from beginning to end not for immediate

---

7. Among the Romans history came to be regarded more as a kind of colorful, artistic, rhetorical, literary, and ethical form than as the severely accurate factual, unbiased, scientific work which we expect it to be. Ideally, historical composition should seek to combine literary form with scientific accuracy.

effect or the instant necessities of forensic strife, but to record events for the benefit of posterity and to win glory for its author. Consequently, to avoid monotony of narrative, it employs unusual words and indulges in a freer use of figures. There is, it is true, another advantage which we may derive from the historians, which, however, despite its great importance, has no bearing on our present topic;[8] I refer to the advantage derived from the knowledge of historical facts and precedents, with which it is most desirable that our orator should be acquainted; for such knowledge will save him from having to acquire all his evidence from his client and will enable him to draw much that is germane to his case from the careful study of antiquity. And such arguments will be all the more effective, since they alone will be above suspicion of prejudice or partiality.[9]

X.i.35-36. Read philosophy.

The fact that there is so much for which we must have recourse to the study of the philosophers is the fault of orators who have abandoned to them the fullest portion of their own task. The Stoics more especially discourse and argue with great keenness on what is just, honourable, expedient and the reverse, as well as on the problems of theology, while the Socratics[10] give the future orator a first-rate preparation for forensic debates and the examination of witnesses. But we must use the same critical caution in studying the philosophers that we require in reading history or poetry; that is to say, we must bear in mind that, even when we are dealing with the same subjects, there is a wide difference between forensic disputes and philosophical discussions, between the law-courts and the lecture-room, between the precepts of theory and the perils of the bar.

X.i.37-44. Ancient authors who have stood the test of time, and modern authors, whom we have to test for ourselves—hardly any author will fail to be of some use.

Most of my readers will, I think, demand that since I attach so much importance to reading, I should include in this work some

---

8. I.e., the oratorical power and sure facility stated in X.i.1 above.

9. This passage demonstrates the great value of historical perspective; for, since it is based on a knowledge of things already done and experiences already gained, it provides arguments and evidence "above suspicion of prejudice or partiality." Such is the perspective provided by a reading of Quintilian.

10. Socrates was famous for his dialectic method (logical discussion) and cross-examinations.

instructions as to what authors should be read and what their special excellences may be. To do this in detail would be an endless task. Remember that Cicero in his *Brutus,* after writing pages and pages on the subject of Roman orators alone, says nothing of his own contemporaries with the exception of Caesar and Marcellus. What limit, then, would there be to my labours if I were to attempt to deal with them and with their successors and all the orators of Greece as well? No, it was a safer course that Livy adopted in his letter to his son, where he writes that he should read Cicero and Demosthenes and then such orators as resembled them. Still, I must not conceal my own personal convictions on this subject. I believe that there are few, indeed scarcely a single one of those authors who have stood the test of time who will not be of some use or other to judicious students, since even Cicero himself admits that he owes a great debt even to the earliest writers, who for all their talent were totally devoid of art. And my opinion about the moderns is much the same. For how few of them are so utterly crazy as not to have the least shadow of hope that some portion or other of their work may have claims upon the memory of posterity? If there is such an one, he will be detected before we have perused many lines of his writings, and we shall escape from him before the experiment of reading him has cost us any serious loss of time. On the other hand, not everything that has some bearing on some department of knowledge will necessarily be of service for the formation of style, with which we are for the moment concerned.

Before, however, I begin to speak of individual authors, I must make a few general remarks about the variety of judgments which have been passed upon them. For there are some who think that only the ancients should be read and hold that they are the sole possessors of natural eloquence and manly vigour; while others revel in the voluptuous and affected style of to-day, in which everything is designed to charm the ears of the uneducated majority. For the moment I shall restrict myself to touching briefly on what the student who desires to consolidate his powers of speaking should seek in his reading and to what kind of reading he should devote his attention. My design is merely to select a few of the most eminent authors for consideration.[11]

11. Quintilian devotes the rest of Chapter i of Book X to his famous review of important Greek and Roman authors whose works provide particularly good reading for the orator and his rhetoric.

Chapter iii. Writing (composition), its importance and practice.
X.iii.1-4. Cicero called writing "the best producer and teacher of eloquence." We must write as much as possible and with utmost care.

Such are the aids which we may derive from external sources; as regards those which we must supply for ourselves, it is the pen which brings at once the most labour and the most profit. Cicero is fully justified in describing it as the best producer and teacher of eloquence, and it may be noted that in the *de Oratore* he supports his own judgment by the authority of Lucius Crassus, in whose mouth he places this remark. We must therefore write as much as possible and with the utmost care. For as deep ploughing makes the soil more fertile for the production and support of crops, so, if we improve our minds by something more than mere superficial study, we shall produce a richer growth of knowledge and shall retain it with greater accuracy. For without the consciousness of such preliminary study our powers of speaking extempore will give us nothing but an empty flow of words, springing from the lips and not from the brain. It is in writing that eloquence has its roots and foundations, it is writing that provides that holy of holies where the wealth of oratory is stored, and whence it is produced to meet the demands of sudden emergencies. It is of the first importance that we should develop such strength as will not faint under the toil of forensic strife nor be exhausted by continual use. For it is an ordinance of nature that nothing great can be achieved in a moment,[12] and that all the fairest tasks are attended with difficulty, while on births as well she has imposed this law, that the larger the animal, the longer should be the period of gestation.

X.iii.4-10. At first write slowly and carefully, and revise frequently. Speed will come with practice.

There are, however, two questions which present themselves in this connexion, namely, what should be our method and what the subjects on which we write, and I propose to treat them in this order. At first, our pen must be slow yet sure: we must search for what is best and refuse to give a joyful welcome to every thought

12. Once again that very sage advice "slow but sure," *festina lente*, which is just as valid and just as much needed today as it was in Quintilian's time. Let us be thorough in our educating; and let us help our students to lay firm, sound foundations which will remain good and reliable for the rest of their lives. Cheap and shoddy foundations will quickly crumble. We need human edifices built on a rock.Cp. §§5-10 below; also I.i.32 above and note 15 thereon, I.iv.5 and II.iv.17.

the moment that it presents itself; we must first criticise the fruits of our imagination, and then, once approved, arrange the fruits of our imagination, and then, once approved, arrange them with care. For we must select both thoughts and words and weigh them one by one. This done, we must consider the order in which they should be placed, and must examine all the possible varieties of rhythm, refusing necessarily to place each word in the order in which it occurs to us. In order to do this with the utmost care, we must frequently revise what we have just written.[13] For besides the fact that thus we secure a better connexion between what follows and what precedes, the warmth of thought which has cooled down while we were writing is revived anew, and gathers fresh impetus from going over the ground again. But we must give them a critical revision, and go carefully over any passage where we have reason to regard our fluency with suspicion. It is thus, we are told, that Sallust[14] wrote, and certainly his works give clear evidence of the labour which he expended on them. Again, we learn from Varius that Virgil composed but a very small number of verses every day.[15] I is true that with orators the case is somewhat different, and it is for this reason that I enjoin such slowness of speed and such anxious care at the outset. For the first aim which we must fix in our minds and insist on carrying into execution is to write as well as possible; speed will come with practice. Gradually thoughts will suggest themselves with increasing readiness, the words will answer to our call and rhythmical arrangement will follow, till everything will be found

13. Anyone who has done any careful writing should be well aware how correct Quintilian is throughout this passage in the matter of rereading, revising, and rewriting. This is one of the best pieces of advice that any teacher can take to heart for himself or recommend to students for success in preparing a paper or a book. The Roman poet Horace, whom J. W. Duff calls "the foe of slip-shod genius," says in *Satires*, I.X.72-73: "Often invert your pencil [i.e., erase, correct, revise] if you intend to write something worthy to be read a second time." One also thinks of Horace's *labor limae*, "the labor of the file," i.e., revision and polishing (*Ars Poetica* 291). This is all part of Quintilian's emphasis on thoroughness and discipline without which there is no excellence—a message for our rather shoddy times and the cult of the unkempt. See also X.iv.1 below and note 21 thereon.

14. Sallust, a Roman historian of the first century B.C., was noted for his terse, rapid, epigrammatic style.

15. Varius, himself a distinguished poet, was Virgil's literary executor. Virgil's unhurried, meticulous, perfectionistic method of composition produced only a very few lines a day which satisfied his own severe standards, but this method resulted in the *Aeneid*, Rome's greatest epic and one of the world's greatest epics.

fulfilling its proper function as in a well-ordered household. The sum of the whole matter is this: write quickly and you will never write well, write well and you will soon write quickly.[16]

X.iii.10-15. However, we should not be so critical of ourselves as to become impotent; practice is essential but we need judgment as well.

But it is just when we have acquired this facility that we must pause awhile to look ahead and, if I may use the metaphor, curb the horses that would run away with us. This will not delay our progress so much as lend us fresh vigour. For I do not think that those who have acquired a certain power in writing should be condemned to the barren pains of false self-criticism. How can anyone fulfill his duties as an advocate if he wastes his time in putting unnecessary finish on each portion of his pleadings? There are some who are never satisfied. They wish to change everything they have written and to put it in other words. They are a diffident folk, and deserve but ill of their own talents, who think it a mark of precision to cast obstacles in the way of their own writing. Nor is it easy to say which are the most serious offenders, those who are satisfied with everything or those who are satisfied with nothing that they write. For it is of common occurrence with young men, however talented they may be, to waste their gifts by superfluous elaboration, and to sink into silence through an excessive desire to speak well. I remember in this connexion a story that Julius Secundus, my contemporary, and, as is well known, my very dear friend, a man with remarkable powers of eloquence, but with an infinite passion for precision, told me of the words once used to him by his uncle, Julius Florus, the leading orator of Gaul, for it was there that he practised, a man eloquent as but few have ever been, and worthy of his nephew. He once noticed that Secundus, who was still a student, was looking depressed, and asked him the meaning of his frowns. The youth made no concealment of the reason: he had been working for three days, and had been unable, in spite of all his efforts, to devise an exordium for the theme which he had been given to write, with the result that he was not only vexed over his immediate difficulty, but had lost all hope of future success. Florus smiled and said, "Do you really want to speak better than

---

16. This summarizing epigram beautifully reproduces the epigrammatic quality of Quintilian's own Latin here. Cp. II.iv.17 re learning to speak well before trying to speak rapidly.

you can?" There lies the truth of the whole matter. We must aim at speaking as well as we can, but must not try to speak better than our nature will permit. For to make any real advance we need study, not self-accusation. And it is not merely practice that will enable us to write at greater length and with increased fluency, although doubtless practice is most important. We need judgment as well. So long as we do not lie back with eyes turned up to the ceiling, trying to fire our imagination by muttering to ourselves, in the hope that something will present itself, but turn our thoughts to consider what the circumstances of the case demand, what suits the character involved, what is the nature of the occasion and the temper of the judge, we shall acquire the power of writing by rational means. It is thus that nature herself bids us begin and pursue our studies once well begun.

X.iii.22-29. Best conditions for writing and study: seclusion and silence, good health, freedom from fatigue, power of concentration. We must avoid pretexts for idleness.

Everyone will agree that the absence of company and deep silence are most conducive to writing, though I would not go so far as to concur in the opinion of those who think woods and groves the most suitable localities for the purpose, on the ground that the freedom of the sky and the charm of the surroundings produce sublimity of thought and wealth of inspiration.[17] Personally I regard such an environment as a pleasant luxury rather than a stimulus to study. For whatever causes us delight, must necessarily distract us from the concentration due to our work. The mind cannot devote its undivided and sincere attention to a number of things at the same time, and wherever it turns its gaze it must cease to contemplate its appointed task. Therefore, the charm of the woods, the gliding of the stream, the breeze that murmurs in the branches, the song of birds, and the very freedom with which our eyes may range, are mere distractions, and in my opinion the pleasure which they excite is more likely to relax than to concentrate our attention. Demosthenes took a wiser view; for he would retire to a place where no voice was to be

---

17. Pliny the Younger, illustrious pupil of Quintilian, in one of his letters (*Epistles*, 1.6) expresses ideas closely parallel to those stated here about composing out in the "woods and groves." Somewhat similarly on delicious spring days modern students have been known to ask that the class be held out of doors on the campus lawn under the trees. With his characteristic common sense Quintilian suggests that this sort of thing is more for pleasure than for work.

(Reading and Writing) Bk. X.iii

heard, and no prospect greeted the sight, for fear that his eyes might force his mind to neglect its duty. Therefore, let the burner of the midnight oil[18] seclude himself in the silence of night, within closed doors, with but a solitary lamp to light his labours. But for every kind of study, and more especially for night work, good health and its chief source, simple living, are essential; for we have fallen into the habit of devoting to relentless labour the hour which nature has appointed for rest and relaxation.[19] From those hours we must take only such time as is superfluous for sleep, and will not be missed. For fatigue will make us careless in writing, and the hours of daylight are amply sufficient for one who has no other distractions. It is only the busy man who is driven to encroach on the hours of darkness. Nevertheless, night work, so long as we come to it fresh and untired, provides by far the best form of privacy.

But although silence and seclusion and absolute freedom of mind are devoutly to be desired, they are not always within our power to attain. Consequently we must not fling aside our book at once, if disturbed by some noise, and lament that we have lost a day: on the contrary, we must make a firm stand against such inconveniences, and train ourselves so to concentrate[20] our thoughts as to rise superior to all impediments to study. If only you direct all your attention to the work which you have in hand, no sight or sound will ever penetrate to your mind. If even casual thoughts often occupy us to such an extent that we do not see passers-by, or even stray from our path, surely we can obtain the same result by the exercise of our will. We must not give way to pretexts for sloth. For unless we make up our mind that we must be fresh, cheerful and free from all other care when we approach our studies, we shall always find some excuse for idleness.

X.iv.1-4. Correction or revision as the most useful part of our studies; the best method. However, let us not overdo it.

18. I.e., olive oil, which provided the most common form of illumination by means of the Roman lamp, so many examples of which are to be seen in our museums. Actually this illumination was poor and unsteady according to our standards.

19. Again note Quintilian's sound common sense throughout this passage.

20. Concentration is still a problem with us today as it was with the Romans. Since it has unquestionably been at the root of many academic failures, teachers should contrive as many devices as possible to help their students develop the power of concentration, for once acquired this power can prove one of the great aids to success throughout life.

The next point which we have to consider is the correction of 1
our work, which is by far the most useful portion of our study:
for there is good reason for the view that erasure is quite as
important a function of the pen[21] as actual writing. Correction
takes the form of addition, excision and alteration. But it is a
comparatively simple and easy task to decide what is to be added
or excised. On the other hand, to prune what is turgid, to elevate
what is mean, to repress exuberance, arrange what is disorderly,
introduce rhythm where it is lacking, and modify it where it is too
emphatic, involves a twofold labour. For we have to condemn
what had previously satisfied us and discover what had escaped
our notice. There can be no doubt that the best method of 2
correction is to put aside what we have written for a certain time,[22]
so that when we return to it after an interval it will have the air of
novelty and of being another's handiwork; for thus we may prevent ourselves from regarding our writings with all the affection
that we lavish on a newborn child. But this is not always possible, 3
especially in the case of an orator who most frequently has to write
for immediate use, while some limit, after all, must be set to
correction. For there are some who return to everything they
write with a presumption that it is full of faults, and, assuming
that a first draft must necessarily be incorrect, think every change
an improvement and make some alteration as often as they have
the manuscript in their hands: they are, in fact, like doctors who
use the knife even when the flesh is perfectly healthy. The result

21. As was stated in note 4 on I.i.27 above, "pencil" could be a better, though less poetic, translation of *stilus* (our word *stylus*), the pointed end of which was used to write (engrave) on wax tablets, while the opposite and rounded end was used to smooth out and obliterate any undesirable incised writing, and so to erase. (*Calamus* was a pen in our sense, used to write with ink on paper or parchment.) Cp. Horace's advice about "inverting the stilus" as quoted in note 13 on X.iii.6 above.

22. Similarly Horace in *Ars Poetica* line 388 suggests that one put his literary work aside for nine years to let it mellow before publication. This ancient device of rereading and revising after an interval is no less valid today than it was for Quintilian, as many a writer will testify. In humble terms, for instance, countless difficult, often mean, letters have been mercifully altered for the better by even so brief an interval as the next day's rereading and revision. Let teachers exhort their students to follow Quintilian's wise advice in the writing of compositions, reports, and all other papers. Even though this passage and note are somewhat reminiscent of X.iii.6 and note 13 above, each gains emphasis from referral to the other. However, note in §§ 3 and 4 Quintilian's reasonableness in not pushing a good point too far.

(Reading and Writing) Bk. X.iv, v

of their critical activities is that the finished work is full of scars, bloodless, and all the worse for their anxious care. No! Let there be something in all our writing which, if it does not actually please us, at least passes muster, so that the file may only polish our work, not wear it away. There must also be a limit to the time which we spend on its revision.

X.v.1-3. Translation, a valuable exercise for writing.

My next task is to indicate what those should write whose aim is to acquire facility.[23] At this part of my work there is no necessity for me to set forth the subjects which should be selected for writing, or the order in which they should be approached, since I have already done this in the first book,[24] where I prescribed the sequence of studies for boys, and in the second book,[25] where I did the same for young men. The point which concerns me now is to show from what sources copiousness and facility may most easily be derived.

Our earlier orators thought highly of translation from Greek into Latin.[26] In the *de Oratore*[27] of Cicero, Lucius Crassus says that he practised this continually, while Cicero himself advocates it

23. See X.i.1.
24. See I.ix.
25. See II.iv.
26. As background for this statement let us recall that the educated Romans were bilingual, speaking and reading and writing Greek about as well as they did their own native Latin. Yet Quintilian here cites famous Roman orators who thought that translation was an excellent exercise; and Pliny (*Epistles*, VII.9.2) in similar words says that it is extremely useful to translate from Greek into Latin or from Latin to Greek, and he adds that many recommend this. In essence both Quintilian and Pliny are saying that this experience teaches more about one's own mother tongue and teaches it more precisely, rigorously, effectively than most other exercises, and it improves one's understanding, judgment, and power of expression. From this ancient experience one can deduce how valuable translation is for the improvement and the appreciation of our own English today —translation, from any language but especially from Latin for a number of reasons. This can also and should always be made a humanistic experience. All this refutes the currently fashionable educationists who glibly seek to throw foreign language study out of the curriculum on the pretext of irrelevancy or perhaps, in fact, because in our too frequently soft academic times it is more intellectually demanding than some people wish. Finally, without denying the need for some amount of reasonable change, one thinks of those language teachers themselves who, taking an extreme posture, would jettison the tried and tested translation method totally as an anathema and would rely solely on new-fangled methods and machines.
27. *De Oratore*, I.34.155.

again and again, nay, he actually published translations of Xenophon and Plato,[28] which were the result of this form of exercise. Messala likewise gave it his approval, and we have a number of translations of speeches from his hand.[29] The purpose of this form of exercise is obvious. For Greek authors are conspicuous for the variety of their matter, and there is much art in all their eloquence, while, when we translate them, we are at liberty to use the best words available, since all that we use are our very own.[30] As regards figures, too, which are the chief ornament of oratory, it is necessary to think out a great number and variety for ourselves, since in this respect the Roman idiom differs largely from the Greek.

X.vii.7-8. *Speaking extempore; frequent practice.*

We must acquire a store of the best words and phrases on lines that I have already laid down, while our style must be formed by continuous and conscientious practice in writing, so that even our improvisations may reproduce the tone of our writing, and after writing much, we must give ourselves frequent practice in speaking. For facility is mainly the result of habit and exercise.

---

28. The *Oeconomicus* of Xenophon and the *Protagoras* and *Timaeus* of Plato.

29. Although Messala (late first century B.C., Augustan period) was a distinguished orator, scholar, poet, patron, soldier, statesman, his works have not survived.

30. In the next few omitted sections Quintilian praises as a valuable exercise the composing in Latin of paraphrases of Latin works, especially poetry. However, we see here in this present section that translating from Greek into Latin is a much better exercise and discipline because obviously there are no Latin words (as in paraphrasing Latin works) to give the Roman student even a hint of the expression which he might use; and so the translator is completely on his own to determine the best words and expression. This corroborates note 26 above.

BOOK XI

EXCERPTS FROM CHAPTER II

(Memory)

XI.ii.1. Memory: our whole education depends on memory!

Some regard memory as being no more than one of nature's gifts; and this view is no doubt true to a great extent; but, like everything else, memory may be improved by cultivation. And all the labour of which I have so far spoken will be in vain unless all the other departments be co-ordinated by the animating principle of memory. For our whole education depends upon memory, and we shall receive instruction all in vain if all we hear slips from us, while it is the power of memory alone that brings before us all the store of precedents, laws, rulings, sayings and facts which the orator must possess in abundance and which he must always hold ready for immediate use. Indeed it is not without good reason that memory has been called the treasure-house of eloquence.[1]

XI.ii.27-31,33. A few of Quintilian's mnemonic devices: symbols, ring, string, names; memorize via mind, voice, and ear.

If a speech of some length has to be committed to memory, it will be well to learn it piecemeal, since there is nothing so bad for the memory as being overburdened. But the sections into which we divide it for this purpose should not be very short; otherwise they will be too many in number, and will break up and distract the memory. I am not, however, prepared to recommend any

---

1. See Book II.vii.2-4 above and note 46 thereon.

definite length; it will depend on the natural limits of the passage concerned, unless, indeed, it be so long as itself to require subdivision. But some limits must be fixed to enable us, by dint of frequent and continuous practice, to connect the words in their proper order, which is a task of no small difficulty, and subsequently to unite the various sections into a whole when we go over them in order. If certain portions prove especially difficult to remember, it will be found advantageous to indicate them by certain marks, the remembrance of which will refresh and stimulate the memory. For there can be but few whose memory is so barren that they will fail to recognise the symbols with which they have marked different passages. But if anyone is slow to recognize his own signs, he should employ the following additional remedy, which, though drawn from the mnemonic system discussed above, is not without its uses: he will adapt his symbols to the nature of the thoughts which tend to slip from his memory, using an anchor, as I suggested above, if he has to speak of a ship, or a spear, if he has to speak of a battle. For symbols are highly efficacious, and one idea suggests another: for example, if we change a ring from one finger to another or tie a thread round it, it will serve to remind us of our reason for so doing. Specially effective are those devices which lead the memory from one thing to another similar thing which we have got to remember; for example, in the case of names, if we desire to remember the name Fabius, we should think of the famous Cunctator,[2] whom we are certain not to forget, or of some friend bearing the same name. This is specially easy with names such as Aper, Ursus, Naso, or Crispus,[3] since in these cases we can fix their origin in our memory.

The question has been raised as to whether we should learn by heart in silence; it would be best to do so, save for the fact that under such circumstances the mind is apt to become indolent, with the result that other thoughts break in. For this reason the mind should be kept alert by the sound of the voice, so that the

2. Quintus Fabius Maximus was given the sobriquet of Cunctator, the Delayer, because after Hannibal had slaughtered a number of Roman armies in pitched battles, Fabius as the new Roman general saved Rome for a time by his tactics of delay in refusing to confront Hannibal in open battle, while he safely harassed him by exasperating forays. Hence, incidentally, the Fabian socialism of the Fabian Society.

3. Meaning respectively: Boar, Bear, Nose, Curly.

(Memory) Bk. XI.ii

XI.ii.40-42. The supreme method of memory is practice and industry. Children should learn as much as possible by heart.

However, if anyone asks me what is the one supreme method of memory, I shall reply, practice and industry. The most important thing is to learn much by heart, and to think much, and, if possible, to do this daily, since there is nothing that is more increased by practice or impaired by neglect than memory. Therefore boys should, as I have already urged,[4] learn as much as possible by heart at the earliest stage, while all who, whatever their age, desire to cultivate the power of memory, should endeavour to swallow the initial tedium of reading and re-reading what they have written or read, a process which we may compare to chewing the cud. This task will be rendered less tiresome if we begin by confining ourselves to learning only a little at a time, in amounts not sufficient to create disgust: we may then proceed to increase the amount by a line a day, an addition which will not sensibly increase the labour of learning, until at last the amount we can attack will know no limits. We should begin with poetry and then go to oratory, while finally we may attempt passages still freer in rhythm and less akin to ordinary speech, such, for example, as passages from legal writers. For passages intended as an exercise should be somewhat difficult in character if they are to make it easy to achieve the end for which the exercise is designed; just as athletes train the muscles of their hands by carrying weights of lead, although in the contests their hands will be empty and free.

---

4. See Book I.i.36 and II.vii.2-4 above.

BOOK XII

EXCERPTS FROM CHAPTERS I, II, AND XI

(The Character of the Ideal Orator)

XII.i.1. The orator is "a good man skilled in speaking."

The orator then, whom I am concerned to form, shall be the orator as defined by Marcus Cato, "a good man, skilled in speaking."[1] But above all he must possess the quality which Cato places first and which is in the very nature of things the greatest and most important, that is, he must be a good man. This is essential not merely on account of the fact that, if the powers of eloquence serve only to lend arms to crime, there can be nothing more pernicious than eloquence to public and private welfare alike, while I myself, who have laboured to the best of my ability to contribute something of value to oratory, shall have rendered the worst of services to mankind, if I forge these weapons not for a soldier, but for a robber.[2]

XII.i.25-31. An inspiring picture of the ideal orator as a good man.

It is no hack-advocate, no hireling pleader, nor yet, to use no harsher term, a serviceable attorney of the class generally known as *causidici*,[3] that I am seeking to form, but rather a man who to

---

1. Cp. Book I.Pref.9.
2. Cp. II.xvi.1-10 *et passim.* Cp. also Cicero, *de Oratore,* III.14.55: "For if we bestow the faculty of eloquence on people destitute of these virtues, we shall not make them orators, mind you, but give arms, as it were, to madmen."

3. *Causidicus,* literally = "a case pleader," a pettifogger, an advocate primarily interested in his fees and regarded as inferior to the orator.

(The Character of the Ideal Orator) Bk. XII.i

extraordinary natural gifts has added a thorough mastery of all the fairest branches of knowledge, a man sent by heaven to be the blessing of mankind, one to whom all history can find no parallel, uniquely perfect in every detail and utterly noble alike in thought and speech.[4] How small a portion of all these abilities will be required for the defence of the innocent, the repression of crime or the support of truth against falsehood in suits involving question of money? It is true that our supreme orator will bear his part in such tasks, but his powers will be displayed with brighter splendour in greater matters than these, when he is called upon to direct the counsels of the senate and guide the people from the paths of error to better things. Was not this the man conceived by Virgil and described as quelling a riot when torches and stones have begun to fly:[5]

"Then, if before their eyes some statesman grave
Stand forth, with virtue and high service crowned,
Straight are they dumb and stand intent to hear."

Here then we have one who is before all else a good man, and it is only after this that the poet adds that he is skilled in speaking:

"His words their minds control, their passions soothe."

Again, will not this same man, whom we are striving to form, if in time of war he be called upon to inspire his soldiers with courage for the fray, draw for his eloquence on the innermost precepts of philosophy? For how can men who stand upon the verge of battle banish all the crowding fears of hardship, pain, and death from their minds, unless those fears be replaced by the sense of the duty that they owe their country, by courage and the lively image of a soldier's honour? And assuredly the man who will best inspire such feelings in others is he who has first inspired them in

---

4. Cp. I. Pref.9-13.

5. Virgil, *Aeneid*, Book I.151-153. Virgil uses this very vivid and powerful simile to illustrate how Neptune, mighty god of the sea, had just calmed the howling winds and crashing waves which had nearly obliterated Aeneas' fleet. The preceding three lines (148-150) are worth giving here as a background for the lines quoted by Quintilian and also because they reflect only too vividly many ugly scenes in our own recent experience when we should have welcomed just such a great and effective orator-statesman as Quintilian and Virgil had in mind: "and just as when often a riot develops in a large gathering of people and the common throng rage in their souls, and soon rocks and firebrands fly and their frenzy supplies arms, then. . ." Notice the implication that this great man could not have controlled the people without the power and influence both of his character (he was "a good man") and of his well-disciplined words ("skilled in speaking").

himself. For however we strive to conceal it, insincerity will always betray itself,[6] and there was never in any man so great eloquence as would not begin to stumble and hesitate so soon as his words ran counter to his inmost thoughts. Now a bad man cannot help speaking things other than he feels. On the other hand, the good will never be at a loss for honourable words or fail to find matter full of virtue for utterance, since among his virtues practical wisdom will be one. And even though his imagination lacks artifice to lend it charm, its own nature will be ornament enough, for if honour dictate the words, we shall find eloquence there as well. Therefore, let those that are young, or rather let all of us, whatever our age, since it is never too late to resolve to follow what is right, strive with all our hearts and devote all our efforts to the pursuit of virtue and eloquence; and perchance it may be granted to us to attain to the perfection that we seek.

XII.ii.1-8. Formation of the orator's character is paramount; and the orator must carefully observe the influence of nature and form his character on the precepts of philosophy and the dictates of reason.

Since then the orator is a good man, and such goodness cannot be conceived as existing apart from virtue, virtue, despite the fact that it is in part derived from certain natural impulses, will require to be perfected by instruction. The orator must above all things devote his attention to the formation of moral character and must acquire a complete knowledge of all that is just and honourable. For without this knowledge no one can be either a good man or skilled in speaking, unless indeed we agree with those who regard morality as intuitive and as owing nothing to instruction: indeed they go so far as to acknowledge that handicrafts, not excluding even those which are most despised among them, can only be acquired by the result of teaching, whereas virtue, which of all gifts to man is that which makes him most near akin to the immortal gods, comes to him without search or effort, as a natural concomitant of birth. But can the man who does not know what abstinence is, claim to be truly abstinent? Or brave, if he has never purged his soul of the fears of pain, death and superstition? Or just, if he has never, in language approaching that of philosophy, discussed the nature of virtue and justice, or of the laws that have been given to mankind by nature or estab-

---

6. One is reminded of the statement "What you are speaks so loudly that I cannot hear what you say."

(The Character of the Ideal Orator) Bk. XII.i, ii

lished among individual peoples and nations? What a contempt it argues for such themes to regard them as being so easy of comprehension! However, I pass this by; for I am sure that no one with the least smattering of literary culture will have the slightest hesitation in agreeing with me. I will proceed to my next point, that no one will achieve sufficient skill even in speaking, unless he makes a thorough study of all the workings of nature and forms his character on the precepts of philosophy and the dictates of reason. For it is with good cause that Lucius Crassus, in the third book of the *de Oratore*,[7] affirms that all that is said concerning equity, justice, truth and the good, and their opposites, forms part of the studies of an orator, and that the philosophers, when they exert their powers of speaking to defend these virtues, are using the weapons of rhetoric, not their own. But he also confesses that the knowledge of these subjects must be sought from the philosophers for the reason that, in his opinion, philosophy has more effective possession of them. And it is for the same reason that Cicero in several of his books and letters proclaims that eloquence has its fountain-head in the most secret springs of wisdom, and that consequently for a considerable time the instructors of morals and of eloquence were identical.[8]

Accordingly this exhortation of mine must not be taken to mean that I wish the orator to be a philosopher, since there is no other way of life that is further removed from the duties of a statesman and the tasks of an orator. For what philosopher has ever been a frequent speaker in the courts or won renown in public assemblies? Nay, what philosopher has ever taken a prominent part in the government of the state, which forms the most frequent theme of their instructions? None the less I desire that he, whose character I am seeking to mould, should be a "wise man"[9] in the Roman sense, that is, one who reveals himself as a

---

7. Cicero, *de Oratore*, III. 20,27,31.
8. Cp. Quintilian I, Preface 13-14 and note 5 thereon, also II.iii.12 and note 20 thereon re Phoenix.
9. The Greek word *philosophos* means "a lover of wisdom *(sophia)*"; and *sophia*, though originally more or less practical, tended to become in the Greek fashion increasingly abstract and theoretical. The Latin *sapiens*, "wise" or a "wise man," was sometimes used by the Romans as equivalent to philosopher; but while Quintilian wanted his ideal statesman to be familiar with the theories and ideals of Greek philosophy in its three branches of physics, ethics, and dialectic, the practical Roman in him sought to have his statesman-orator no mere philosopher but a "wise man" in the broadest possible, practical, and active sense of the word.

true statesman, not in the discussions of the study, but in the actual practice and experience of life. But inasmuch as the study of philosophy has been deserted by those who have turned to the pursuit of eloquence, and since philosophy no longer moves in its true sphere of action and in the broad daylight of the forum, but has returned first to porches and gymnasia[10] and finally to the gatherings of the schools,[11] all that is essential for an orator, and yet is not taught by the professors of eloquence, must undoubtedly be sought from those persons in whose possessions it has remained. The authors who have discoursed on the nature of virtue must be read through and through, that the life of the orator may be wedded to the knowledge of things human and divine.

XII.xi.30-31. Conclusion.

Wherefore let us seek with all our hearts that true majesty of oratory, the fairest gift of god to man, without which all things are stricken dumb and robbed alike of present glory and the immortal record of posterity; and let us press forward to whatsoever is best, since, if we do this, we shall either reach the summit or at least see many others far beneath us.

Such, Marcellus Victorius, were the views by the expression of which it seemed to me that I might, as far as in me lay, help to advance the teaching of oratory. If the knowledge of these principles proves to be of small practical utility to the young student, it should at least produce what I value more,—the will to do well.

Wouldn't this be an excellent ideal also for the modern, well-educated teacher whatever his position in the country's educational system?

10. Porches, or porticoes (stoas in Greek), and gymnasia were surprisingly versatile structures where a variety of mundane and cultural activities occurred. In the Painted Stoa in Athens the philosopher Zeno used to meet with his followers and thus his philosophy came to be known as the philosophy of the stoa or Stoic Philosophy. Two of the most important gymnasia at Athens were the Academy and the Lyceum. Plato conducted his classes in the Academy and Aristotle held his in the Lyceum. The derivation of stoic, academy, lyceum, lycée, and the like is easy to see.

11. I.e., schools of philosophy which developed during the later Hellenistic and the Greco-Roman periods such as the later Stoics, the Epicureans, and the New Academy.

Index

Achilles, hero of Homer's *Iliad:* education of, by Phoenix, p.4
Advanced standing, p.79 n.1, II.i.1-6; cp. studying under both a grammaticus and a rhetor at the same time, II.i.12-13
Aristophanes, author of the *Clouds,* a comedy misrepresenting Socrates as a Sophist, teacher of the new education, p.115 n.62
Athens: education at, pp.4-8

Barbarisms: defined and discussed, I.v.5-13; *See also* Solecisms
Bilingualism, of the Romans, I.i.12-14, I.iv.1; the Romans introduced a foreign language (Greek) into the liberal arts curriculum, p. 11; early and concurrent study of Greek and Latin languages and literatures, I.iv.1
Brevity, a virtue in the statement of facts, IV.ii.40-47

Cato, the Censor: Roman author and conservative opposed to Greek influences on Roman education, p. 9; Cato's famous definition of an orator, p.15, XII.i.1; archaic unacceptable words, I.vi.42
Censorship of literature, for younger pupils, I.viii.6-8 and notes 54, 55
Character: *See* s.v. Morality.
Cicero, Marcus Tullius, Rome's greatest orator: Quintilian's fondness for, II.v.20 and n.41; cited as an authority, II.xxi.4-6, 14-15; on translating, X.v.2-3; Cicero's "liberal arts," pp. 16-17; on the lasting delights of literature, p.48 n.28; speeches against corruption, p.116 notes 64, 65; two-year postgraduate study in Greece, p.13; *et passim*
Classes, in Roman schools: classrooms, pp.10-11; lecture classes for literature and rhetoric, I.ii.9-14; problem of too large classes, I.ii.14-16; advantages of classroom instruction, I.ii.17-31
Clearness: the first essential of a good style, II.iii.8 and n.18, VIII.ii.17-23 and n.2; excellence in language means clearness, etc., I.v.1, IV.ii.31-47
Clouds, Aristophanes' comedy involving Socrates and the Sophists, p.115 n.62
Commonplaces: composition exercises defined, II.i.9 and n.6; denounce vices, etc., II.iv.22; *See also* Composition, Theses
Competition: values of, I.i.20, I.ii.18-29; *See* Motivation
Composition (writing): the best producer and teacher of eloquence, X.iii.1-4; importance and practice of, II.vi.1-7, II.vii.2, X.iii in toto; reading as the pilot in composition, X.i.2; topics for compositions, I.ix.1-6, II.i.7-13, II.iv.1-8, II.iv.15-17, 20-25; value of translation, X.v.1-3; importance of correction and revision, X.iii.6-10, X.iv.1-4; best conditions for writing,

X.iii.22-29; *See also* Correction, Declamations

Concentration, in writing and studying, X.iii.22-29

Controversiae: See Declamations

Correction: methods, II.ii.5-7 and n.11, II.iv.8-14, II.vi.3-4; not by flogging, I.iii.13-17 and n.21; need of promptness in correction, I.i.4-11 and n.7, I.v.6-7 and n.38, II.iii.11 and n.19, II.vi.3-4; revision of composition, X.iii.6-10 and notes 13 and 15, X.iv.1-4 and notes 21 and 22; pronunciation, I.xi.4, and 8-14

Courses: *See* Curriculum, Studies

Curriculum: Quintilian's basic curriculum outlined, pp.15-17; elementary (*ludi magister, litterator*), p.10, p.79 n.1, I.i.12-I.iii.18; secondary (*grammaticus*), pp.11-12, p. 71 n.1, I.iv-xi; higher (*rhetor*), pp. 12-13, p.79 n.1, II.iv-xiii; required or optional, well-rounded or narrow, I.x.1 and n.60, I.x.2-8, I.x.30 and n.69, II.viii.1-15; foreign language study introduced by Romans, p.11; *See also* Bilingualism, Studies

Declamations: nature, purpose, methods, II.i.2, II.vi.1-7, II.vii.1-5, II.x.1-15; deliberative themes (*suasoriae*), II.i.2, II.i.8; judicial themes (*controversiae*), II.i.2, II.i.9; commonplaces, II.i.9 and n.6, II.iv.22-23; theses, II.i.9 and n.5, II.iv.24-25; impersonations in character, II.i.2; degeneration of declamation and corruption of oratory, II.x.1-7 and n.54

Discipline (instruction, training, practice, control): acquired by hard work, long study, practice, exercises, revisions, p.3, I.Pref.27 and n.8, I.i.10, I.x.30 and n.69, II.iv.7, II.xiii.15 and n.61; kindly firmness but avoidance of corporal punishment, sarcasm, and undue severity, I.iii.13-18, II.iii.4-8, II.iv.10-14; errors to be corrected at once, I.i.4-11 and n.7, I.v.6-7 and n.38, II.iii.11 and n.19, II.vi.3-4; bombastic rhetors who scorn discipline, II.xi.1-7; the disciplined speaker superior to the undisciplined, II.xii.1-12; further emphasis on excellence, Preface p.VI, Book II.ii.10 and n.12, II.iii.2 and n.16, II.v.10 and n.37, X.i.17-18 and n.5; *See also* Correction, Haste, Revision, Style

Educability, I.i.1-3 and n.1

Education, Greek: outline of, pp.3-8; Greek influence on Roman education, pp. 8-12

Education, Roman: outline of, pp. 8-14; Greek influences, pp. 8-12; purpose and nature of, pp.14-17; value of, I.Pref.10, I.ii.1-3, I.ii.9-16, I.iv.5 and n.28, I.viii.12, I.xii.16-18, II.xxi.5-6, II.xxi.14-19, *et passim;* requisites for success in, I.Pref.27, I.i.10, II.iv.17, II.viii.8; importance of family in, I.i.4-11, I.i.15-20; continuation of, throughout life I.viii.12 and n.56; *See also* such items as Competition, Correction, Curriculum, Discipline, Family, Language, Literature, Liberal Arts, Liberal Education, Methods, Motivation, Parents, Reading

Educational disputes and ferment: conflicting opinions among educators,

Index

I.Pref.1-3; age for beginning a child's education and teaching him to read, I.i.15-20 and n.9; schools or private tutors, I.ii.1-16; discipline by corporal punishment, flogging, I.iii.13-18 and n.21; broad or narrow curriculum, debate over music, geometry, and astronomy, I.x.1-8 and ff.; catering to special talents only, II.viii.1-15; student load and variety in studies, I.xii.1-19; overlapping of grammaticus and rhetor, II.i.1-13; extravagant rhetorical practices of the time, II.x-xiii; the old and the new educations in Aristophanes' *Clouds*, II.xvi.3 n.62; dispute among educators and passion for originality, III.i.5-7,22 (cp. p. 70 n.72); the teaching of Latin, I.iv.22 and n.35

Educational methods: *See* Methods

Errors in speaking and writing, preferably to be avoided, I.i.4-5; to be corrected promptly, I.i.11 and n.7, II.iii.11; errors in pronunciation, I.xi.4 and notes 76, 77; correction and revision in composition, X.iii.6-10, X.iv.1-4; *See also* Correction, Barbarism, Solecism

Etymology: derivation and meaning of, I.vi.28 and n.44; great value of the study of, I.vi.29-31 and n.45

Explication of texts, by explanatory lecturing: in Greek education, p. 5; by grammaticus, I.ii.13-15, I.iv.2, I.viii.8, 13-21; by rhetor, II.v.1-12

Family, importance of in education, I.i.4-11, 15-20; *See also* Parents

Festina lente, make haste slowly, "haste makes waste," "slow but sure": motto of Augustus and a common theme in Quintilian, p.37 n.15, II.iv.17; *See* Discipline, Foundations, Haste

Flogging and similar corporal punishment, denounced by Quintilian, I.iii.13-17 and n.21

Florid school of writing: disapproved of by Quintilian, II.v.18, 22 and n.43

Foreign languages and literatures: not an academic subject for the Greeks, p.11; introduced by the Romans into the curriculum of a liberal education, p.11; *See also* Bilingualism

Foundations, must be carefully and thoroughly laid or the superstructure will collapse, I.iv.5,22 *et passim; See also Festina lente,* Haste

Geometry: as a subject in the secondary curriculum, I.x.2-8; includes mathematics, I.x.34-37 and notes 71,72

Grammatice (techne), the art of speaking and writing correctly and interpreting literature, I.iv.2-5, II.i.1-4 and n.4

Grammaticus, teacher of *grammatice* (q.v.) in the secondary school, commonly translated as "teacher of literature," pp. 9,11-2, 79 n.1; teacher of literature and language, I.ii.14, I.iv.1 and n.23; subjects taught, I.iv.1-9,17-20; lectures by, I.viii.8,13-21; composition taught by, I.ix.1-6; other subjects, I.x

Greek: education, pp.3-8; influence on Roman education, pp. 8-13; Roman boys learned both Greek and Latin, I.i.12-14 and n.8, I.iv.1; Cicero on translating from Greek into Latin, X.v.2-3

Gymnastic, athletic training very important in Greek education, pp. 4-5; not quite so important in Roman education, p.11, I.xi.15-19

Haste, admonitions against undue haste: too great haste in reading, I.i.32-33; foundations to be carefully laid, I.iv.5; haste and short cuts delay progress, I.iv.22; learn to speak correctly before trying to speak rapidly, II.iv.15-17; write slowly and carefully, speed comes with practice, X.iii.4-10 and n.12; *See Festina lente,* Discipline, Foundations

History, its value for study and perspective: explication of historical narratives, I.viii.18; historical narrative as a rhetorical exercise, II.iv.2-5; Roman concept of history, X.i.31 and n.7; value of reading history, X.i.31,34 and n.9

Home, very important in a child's experience: among the Greeks parents, nurse, and paedagogus important for morals, manners, and religion, p. 5; Roman father as teacher in earliest times, p. 9; preschool activity at home, p.10; qualifications of parents, nurse, and paedagogus, I.i.4-11, I.ii.4-5

Homer, Greek epic poet, author of the *Iliad* and *Odyssey,* p. 4; education in Homer, p. 4; ought to be read for greatness of theme and sentiments, I.viii.5; Phoenix as a tutor, p. 4, II.iii.12; even Homer nods, X.i.24; the first line of the *Iliad* shows Homer to have been a "singer," p. 59 n.53

Homework, private study and reading, I.ii.11-12

Humanism, humanists: the humanities — the ancient classical literatures with their humanistic views about man and his morality in this world as compared with the metaphysical interests of medieval Scholasticism, p.14; the humanists of the Renaissance, pp.14,18; liberal arts and the humanities in contradistinction to the sciences, pp.16-17

Imitation, role and value of in education: a sign of educability, I.iii.1; the teacher as a model, II.ii.4-8; models in literature for memorization, I.i.35-36, II.vii.2-4; character molded by contemplation of virtue and vice, II.iv.20; models for imitation supplied by reading, p.16, II.ii.8, X.i.2; power of imitation, X.i.3 and n.2; proper use of poets, X.i.27

Immorality: morals may be corrupted at home, parents' immorality, I.ii.4-8; the problem among students, to be controlled by strict discipline, II.ii.1-4 and n.10, II.ii.14-15; *See* Morality

Isocrates, famous rhetorician of 4th cen. B.C.: stressed many of the ideals found in Quintilian, p.8

Kilpatrick, William Heard: a child should not learn to read before the age of seven, and "progressive" theories, I.i.15 n.9

Language: various aspects and details of language study, I.iv-vii; great value and importance of language as a tool, p.15, II.xvi.11-19 and n.66; excellence in language (e.g., correctness, clearness, elegance), I.v.1, IV.ii.31-47;

Index

proper and vulgar usage discussed, I.i.5 and n.4, I.vi.43-45 and n.47; orthography and usage, I.vii.11,30-31; proper pronunciation, I.xi.4,8; clipping of final syllables (led to Romance languages), I.xi.8 and n.77; easier to learn a language when young, I.xii.9; translation as a valuable exercise for discipline and facility in one's own language, X.v.1-3 and n.26

Lectures, a method of instruction: introduced by Sophists, p. 7; explication of literary texts by the grammaticus, I.ii.13-15, I.iv.2, I.viii.13-15, 17-21; by the rhetor (especially in history and oratory), II.v.1-9,10-12

Liberal arts: derivation of the term and Cicero's "liberal arts," p.16; origin and contents of liberal arts curriculum, pp.16-17; continued throughout the Roman empire and survived as the Seven Liberal Arts of the Middle Ages, pp.13-14; continuation of liberal arts tradition through the Renaissance to our own times, pp.14,17

Liberal education: derivation of the term, p.16; liberal arts curriculum, pp.16-17; literature as a basis of a liberal education and a delight throughout life, I.iv.1-5, I.viii.5-12, I.xii.16-18; *See also* Liberal arts, Literature, Reading

Literature: its value for rhetoric and morality, pp.15-17; cornerstone of a liberal education and a delight throughout life, I.iv.1-5 and n.28, I.viii.5-12; aphorisms and selections from poetry to be memorized by children, I.1.36; value of memorizing selections from orators and historians as models, I.xi.14, II.vii.1-5 and n.46; read critically, X.i.24-25 and n.6

Litterator, p. 47 n.22 (same as *ludi magister* below)

Livius Andronicus, famous for introducing the Greek tradition into Roman education, p. 9

Livy, author of epic-spirited history of Rome, II.v.19 and n.40

Lucretius: 97-53 B.C., Roman epicurean philosopher, author of didactic epic *On the Nature of Things* based on atomic materialism, III.i.4-5 and n.2

Ludus, Latin for elementary school (literally "game," "sport"), p.12; *ludi magister*, schoolmaster, p.10; same as *litterator* above; *See* s.v. Teacher

Mathematics: see Geometry; problem of the new math against the old math, p. 70 n.72

Memory, importance, value, methods: much memorization in Greek education, pp. 5-6; memory as a sign of ability, I.iii.1; memorize much at an early age, I.i.19, I.i.36, XI.ii.41; great value of memorizing selected passages from literature, I.xi.14, II.vii.1-5 and n.46; education of orator depends on memory, XI.ii.1; methods, especially practice and hard work, I.i.31, X.ii.27-33, XI.ii.40-42

Methods, educational: make learning pleasurable for the young, I.i.20,26; alphabet and writing, I.i.24-29, 34-37; syllables, repetition, I.i.30-34; reading, I.i.32-34; private study, I.ii.1 11-12; lectures, *See* Lectures and Explications; periods of relaxation and play, I.iii.8-13; instruction by actors and gym teachers, I.xi.1-4, 8-14,15-19; involve students in classroom exercises,

II.v.6-7 and n.35, II.v.13; methods of correction, *See* Correction and Revision; two methods for composing declamations, II.vi.1-7; different methods for different students, II.viii.1-15; memorization, *See* Memory; *See also* Competition, Motivation, Discipline, Practice, Reading, Work
Models, examples, for rhetoric, morality, etc.: *See* Imitation
Montessori: age at which a child can learn to read, I.i.15-18 and n.9; ivory alphabet letters suggest Montessori's didactic material, I.i.26 and n.10
Morality, character: emphasized in Greek education, pp.4-8; a major theme in Roman education, pp.15-16, I.i.4-11 (re nurse, parents, paedagogos), I.ii.1-8 (home and parents), I.iii.12-13 (games and early formation of character), I.viii.6 (against licentious poetry for the very young); the teacher must be of good character, I.ii.4-5, II.ii.1-4 and n.10, II.ii.13-15; morality through literature and academic exercises, I.i.35-36, I.viii.4, II.iv.20-25 (*See also* Composition, Literature, Reading); good character paramount for the orator, Book XII *passim;* morality in Quintilian's time, I.ii.6-8, II.ii.1-4 and n.10, II.v.12 and n.38
Motivation of students: amusement, competition, praise, rewards, I.i.15-20; comparison, competition, emulation, commendation as stimuli for excellence, I.ii.17-29; study temperaments of different pupils, I.iii.6-9; damage done by dry teachers and undue severity, II.iv.9-11; kind and reasonable treatment and correction according to the student, II.iv.12-14; involving students in classroom exercises, II.v.6-7 and n.35, II.v.13 and n.39; recognition and reward for merit, II.vii.5
Music: whether music should be in the curriculum, I.x.2-8; importance of music in education, I.x.9-10, 14-21; values and powers of music, I.x.22-23; poetry as song, I.viii.2 and n.53

Narrative: among the first rhetorical exercises, II.i.8; three kinds of narrative, all to be composed with utmost care, II.iv.1-7, 15-17; three stylistic virtues of narrative, IV.ii.31-47
Nurse: good character, correct speech, I.i.4-5 and notes 3,4

Obscurity, in style: the worse a teacher is the harder he will be to understand, II.iii.9; extravagant language and verbosity make for obscurity, IV.ii.35-36 and 39, VIII.ii.17-19; obscurity resulting from excessive brevity, IV.ii.44
Orator: the ideal orator as "a good man skilled in speaking," a statesman who devotes himself to the service of his country and whose character is based on philosophy and reason, pp.14-16, I.Pref.9-13, I.xii.16-18, X.i.35-36, XII.i.1,25-31 and n.5, XII.ii.1-8
Oratory: as early as Homer's time, p. 4; especially necessary among the Greeks in the 5th and 4th cens. B.C. (cp. the Sophists), p.7; growing importance in the Roman republic through the 1st cen. B.C. and Greek influences, p.12; Roman oratory less vital under the emperors, pp.12-13; three types of orations, p.13; usefulness of oratory and possible dangers, II.xvi.1-19; corruption of, II.x.1-15 and n.54, II.xi.1-7 and n.56, II.xii.1-12, X.i.18 and n.5;

Index

See also Composition, Rhetoric, Reading, Literature, Language, etc.

Orthography: etymology of, p.57 n.48; discussion of, I.vii.1-4, 11, 30-35; *See also* Spelling

Paedagogus: among the Greeks, p. 5; among the Romans, p. 10; etymology of, p. 31 n.5; duties and responsibilities of, I.i.8-9

Parents: educated as well as possible and diligent about their children, I.i.6-7; great moral responsibility, I.ii.4-5 and n.17; terrific indictment of the irresponsible and corrupt, I.ii.6-8; father responsible for choosing reputable teachers, II.ii.15; sons' ostentatious displays delight fond parents, II.iv.15-16, II.vii.1

Pedagogue: derivation of the word, p. 31 n.5

Pedantry, is to be avoided: in re orthography, I.vii.33-35; by grammaticus in his lectures, I.viii.18-21 and n.58

Philosophy: etymology of, p.151 n.9; Socrates and the philosophical schools, pp.7-8; orator needs virtues discussed by philosophers, I.Pref.9-13, 16-19; grammaticus explicates natural philosophy, I.iv.4 and n.26; orator should read moral philosophy thoroughly, X.i.35-36, XII.ii.18; orator must form character on philosophy and reason, XII.ii.1-8

Phoenix: tutor of Achilles, I.Pref.13 n.5; the teacher should follow his example, II.iii.12 and n.20

Plato, illustrious Greek philosopher of the 4th cen. B.C., disciple of Socrates and teacher of Aristotle: his *Protagoras* tells about Athenian education, pp. 5-6; philosophical school, p. 8

Pliny the Younger, pupil of Quintilian, famous for his letters, p.140 n.17; letter on the value of translation, p.143 n.26

Poetry: extensively read and memorized in Greek schools, pp. 5-6; Roman children memorize, I.i.36; grammaticus interprets, I.iv.3-5; poetry to be read under grammaticus, I.viii.5-12; lectures on poetry by grammaticus, I.viii.13-15, 17-21; poetic license, I.vi.2; poetry is of great service, X.i.27-28

Practice: continuous practice in writing, reading, and speaking, I.Pref.27; practice brings speed in reading, I.i.33; practice strengthens memory, I.i.36; practice more valuable than precept, II.v.15; hard work, study, and practice, II.xiii.15; continued exercise, VIII.Pref.28; diligent practice in writing, with good models, X.i.2-3; speed will come with practice, X.iii.9; translation as practice for writing, X.v.2-3; frequent practice required for facility in speaking, X.vii.7-8; practice and hard work is the supreme method for memory, XI.ii.40

Progressive education: Kilpatrick on the age for learning to read, I.i.15 n.9

Pronunciation: syllables, I.i.30-31, I.i.37; problems with letters, I.i.6-8; orthography and phonetic spelling, I.vii.1-4, 30-32; pronunciation and proper oral delivery, I.xi.4, 8-14

Public schools: at Sparta public and state controlled, at Athens private and by choice of the people, p. 4; at Rome schools "public" in contrast to private

tutors, attendance voluntary but general, p.10, I.ii.1-2 and n.16
Punishment: arguments against flogging and other abuses, I.iii.13-17 and n.21; warning against undue severity in correcting faults, II.iv.10-14
Pupils: memory and imitation as signs of ability, I.iii.1; capacity and treatment of pupils and a picture of the ideal, I.iii; should not be flogged or otherwise mistreated, I.iii.13-17; boys can stand the strain of their studies better than young men, I.xii.1-10; immorality and strict control, I.ii.4-8, II.ii.3-4, 14-15; instruction more acceptable than reproof, but correction is necessary, II.vi.3-4; ideal student-teacher relationship, II.ix.1-3

Quintilian: estimates of, pp.1-2; life and characterization of, pp. 2-3; influence and tradition of, pp.17-19; aim in writing, p.15, I.Pref.9-10; list of some subjects and recurrent themes, especially excellence and detestation of ostentation and sham, Preface pp.V-VI, Introduction pp.1 and 3; vignette of Quintilian at work, II.iv.13-14

Reading: learning to read under the litterator, I.i.30-34; disastrous modern methods of learning to read, p. 36 n.13; broad reading program under the grammaticus, I.iv.1-5, I.viii.5-21; reading program under the rhetor and its values, II.v.18-26; subsequent reading program including speeches, poetry, history, philosophy, p.13, X.i.1-44; reading, writing, and speaking inseparably interconnected, with reading the pilot in composition, X.i.2; reading provides copious vocabulary, X.i.8,10; read thoroughly and critically, X.i.20, 24-26
Relaxation: pupils need relaxation, holidays, games, I.iii.8-12 and n.20
Repetition: repeat syllables to impress them on the memory, I.i.31 and n.14; frequent and continuous practice, XI.ii.28, 40; *et passim*
Revision, of compositions: frequently revise what we have just written, X.iii.6-10 and notes 13 and 15, X.iv.1-4 and notes 21 and 22; *See also* Correction
Rhetor, teacher of rhetoric (q.v.): etymology of *rhetor*, p. 12; a boy may study under both a grammaticus (q.v.) and a rhetor at the same time, II.i.12-13; choice of a teacher of rhetoric, portrait of the ideal teacher, II.ii.1-8; importance of avoiding inferior and dry teachers, II.iii.1-6 and n.16, II.iv.8-14; ostentatious, bombastic rhetors who scorn discipline, II.xi.1-7
Rhetoric, the art of using language effectively in composition and speech: why so necessary for the Greeks and the Romans, pp. 6-8, 9-10, 12-13, 115 n.62; influence of the Greeks on the Romans, pp. 9 and 12; defined as "the power of eloquence," II.i.5; rhetorical exercises, subjects for compositions, II.i.8-12, II.iv.1-8, 15-17, 20-25; rhetorical discipline necessary for effective speaking, II.xi.1-7; the trained speaker superior to the untrained, II.xii.1-12; usefulness and possible dangers of rhetoric, II.xvi.1-19; *See also* Curriculum, Studies, Style, Work, etc.

Index

School, derived from Greek *schole*, literally "leisure" (for learning), p. 12
Socrates: his "Socratic method" and emphasis on virtue and good character, pp. 7-8; Socrates, the Sophists, and Aristophanes' *Clouds*, p. 7, II.xvi.1-3 and n.62; Socrates and the philosophical schools, p.8; approved of oratorical gestures, I.xi.17; on the subject matter of rhetoric, II.xxi.4
Solecisms, substandard or ungrammatical usage: derivation of the term, p. 53 n.40; they, along with barbarisms, not permitted, I.v.5; examples of solecisms discussed, I.v.34, 36-38 and notes 39 and 40
Sophists: brief account of, p.7; *See* Aristophanes' *Clouds* under Socrates
Sparta: education at, in the 5th cen. B.C., p.4
Spelling: orthography (q.v.), I.vii.1-4, 11; preferably phonetic where possible, I.vii.31
Stilus, a pointed instrument for writing on wax tablets, the opposite end rounded to make erasures: used in a groove to teach children to write letters, I.i.27 and n.11; Horace's "invert your stilus" means to erase, correct, revise, X.iii.6 n.13
Students: *See* Pupils
Studies: summary lists of Greek studies, pp.5-6,7,8; lists of Roman studies, pp. 9, 10, 11, 13, I.Pref.21-22, et passim; student load, I.xii.1-19; all studies required except for special cases, II.viii.6-15 and notes 49 and 50; *See also* Curriculum
Style, in composition and speaking: excellence in language is correctness, lucidity, and elegance, I.v.1; clearness is the first essential of good style, II.iii.8 and n.18, VIII.ii.22 and n.2; stylistic virtues in narrative are clearness, brevity, plausibility, IV.ii.31-47 and n.1; barbarisms and solecisms, to be avoided, I.v.5-7; defects in style — affectation, ostentation, extravagance, bombast, verbosity, obscurity, etc., II.v.10-12, 22-26, II.x.1-7 and n.54, II.xi.1-7, IV.ii.39, VIII.ii.17-18, *et passim*
Suasoriae: See Declamations

Teacher: *ludi magister*, or *litterator* — elementary education, pp. 10, 12, 47 n.22, 79 n.1, Book I.i-iii; *grammaticus* — secondary education, pp.11, 79 n.1, I.iv-xii, and *See* s.v. Grammaticus; *rhetor* — higher education, pp.12-13, II.i-xxi, and *See* s.v. Rhetor, Rhetoric; portraits of the ideal teacher, I.ii.15-16, 27 28, I.iii.1, II.ii.1-8, II.iv.8-14, II.viii.1 and n.47; must master every excellence of language, I.v.1; must avoid pedantry and ostentation, I.viii.18-21 and n.58; as a model, see "ideal" above, especially II.ii.4-8; inferior and dry teachers to be avoided, II.iii.1-9, II.iv.8 and n.25; teachers blamed for degeneration of declamation, II.x.3-4 and n.54; censure of irresponsible rhetors who scorn discipline, II.xi.1-7 and n.56, II.xii.1-12; a thorough knowledge of one's subject is more important than mere educational methodology, p. 48 n.27; actors and gym instructors as teachers, I.xi.1-4, 8-19
Teaching: as a vocation, a calling, I.ii.15 and n.19; problem of too large clas-

ses, I.ii.14-16; lecture classes in literature and rhetoric, I.ii.9-14, I.viii.13-21; advantages of classroom instruction as compared with private tutoring, I.ii.17-31

Textbooks: dry textbooks have bad effects, I.Pref.24 and n.7, III.i.1-5 and notes 1 and 2; jejune textbooks which offer merely rigid codes of rules, II.xiii.1-8, 14-17

Thesaurus, treasury, storehouse: literature as a thesaurus for life, p.16; memorize aphorisms and selections from poets as a thesaurus of moral lessons, I.i.36; thesaurus of vocabulary and selections from orators, historians, et al., II.vii.2-4 and n.46; memory, a thesaurus of eloquence, XI.ii.1-2

Thesis: an exercise in composition and declamation, II.i.9 and n.5; composition concerned with a comparison of things, p.81 n.5, II.iv.24-25

Three R's, the: in Greek education, p. 5; in Roman education, p. 9

Translation: Cicero, Pliny, et al. call this a valuable exercise for discipline and facility in one's own language, X.v.1-3 and n.26

Usage: discussion of proper linguistic usage, I.i.5 and n.4, I.vi.43-45; orthography and usage, I.vii.11, 30-31

Virgil, greatest Roman epic poet, author of the *Aeneid:* the power of early habit, I.iii.13; to be read for greatness of theme and sentiments, I.viii.5; poetry is song, p. 59 n.53; his mode of meticulously careful composition, X.iii.8 and n.15; powerful picture of the good orator-statesman, XII.i.27-28 and n.5

Vocabulary: a copious supply of words a prime necessity, VIII.Pref.28 and n.1, II.vii.4, X.i.5-10 and notes 3 and 4, X.vii.7; best acquired by wide reading and continual exercise, VIII.Pref.28 and n.1, X.i.8,10 and n.4; must be used with discrimination, X.i.8

Vocational training: not part of the educational system of the Greeks and Romans, p.16

Work: the gospel of hard work, study, practice, and painstaking, p. 3, II.iv.17, II.xiii.15-17, VIII.Pref.29; work carefully, correct, rework, and revise, p. 90 n.24, X.iii.4,6 and n.13, X.iii.8-10, X.iv.1-4

Writing: learning to write letters of the alphabet quickly and legibly, I.i.25-28 and notes 10,11,12; literary composition; *See* Composition and especially X.iii.1-29